Tax Secrets for Property Developers and Renovators

By

Lee Sharpe

Publisher Details

This guide is published by Tax Portal Ltd. 3 Sanderson Close, Great Sankey, Warrington, Cheshire, WA5 3LN.

'Tax Secrets for Property Developers and Renovators' – First published in July 2006. Second edition April 2007. Third edition May 2008. Fourth edition May 2009. Fifth edition August 2010. Sixth edition May 2011. Seventh edition April 2012. Eighth edition May 2013. Ninth edition April 2014. Tenth edition April 2015. Eleventh edition April 2016.

Contents

About Lee Sharpe

Lee is a Chartered Tax Adviser and tax consultant with over twenty years' experience in helping individuals, families, businesses and advisers with their tax affairs.

Lee writes extensively on tax matters for taxpayers and their advisers, including through the Tax Insider publications, Bloomsbury Professional and the TaxationWeb website. He also lectures taxpayers, accountants and other financial advisers on tax issues.

While he has appeared on TV to comment on tax matters, it was only long enough to establish that he really has a face for radio, and to give fellow members of his local CIOT branch sufficient ammunition with which to embarrass him at committee meetings.

When he is not giving tax advice or writing about tax matters, he is busy looking after his two small children – not because he likes them, but because he wants to make sure that his office is not used exclusively for business purposes…

1   About This Guide

In recent years, there has been a great increase in interest in the property market, and this guide offers advice on the tax pitfalls and opportunities for those who are involved in this dynamic sector.

In particular, it is aimed at:

1.1   Homeowners

All of us who own our own homes hope we are sitting on a goldmine! For many people, their home is their most valuable asset – for some, it is their pension fund!

This section of the guide looks at the tax breaks available to homeowners, and how to get the maximum benefit from them. It also warns of the traps for the unwary!

It is not unusual for a homeowner to find themselves becoming a property developer, perhaps by building another property on their land, or by receiving an offer from a developer to buy their home. We will look at the (sometimes unexpected) ways that such projects are taxed by HM Revenue and Customs (referred to in this guide from now on as HMRC).

1.2   Buy to Let

It seems that these days, everyone is a landlord! In this section, we shall look at the tax treatment of buy to let investors, both on the income from their properties, and on the sale of those properties. We shall cover the letting (and selling) of residential and commercial properties, and that interesting hybrid, furnished holiday accommodation.

1.3   Buy to Sell

Not everyone buys property in order to enjoy the rental income – many intend to turn the properties over quickly by selling them again at a profit.

This sector can be subdivided into three broad categories, all of which we shall look at:

- **"Turnarounds"** These work on the basic commercial principle of "buy cheap and sell dear". A property is bought for a bargain price, perhaps at an auction, and sold on almost immediately, with little or no work done on it to increase its value.

- **"Refurbs"** As the name implies, in a "Refurb", a run-down property is bought, refurbished, and sold – or a large property is bought, converted into smaller units such as flats, and sold.

- **"Property Development"** This can be more or less the same as a refurb, or it may involve buying a vacant plot of land and constructing a new building on it for sale.

2   A Word about Limited Companies

This guide looks at the taxation of individuals who own property, or trade in property, as sole traders or as members of a partnership.

In some cases, it can be advantageous to use a limited company as the vehicle for investing or trading in property – the two commonest examples being:

- If you intend to plough the profits from a rental business back into buying more rental properties, rather than to draw them out for personal expenditure

- If you are a property developer

The decision whether to use a company or not can be a very difficult one, and it is beyond the scope of this guide.

If you would like detailed information and advice about whether a limited company would be the best way forward for your business, our guide "**Tax Dos and Don'ts of Property Companies**" is available from www.property-tax-portal.co.uk. Between the two of them, they offer a comprehensive guide to tax for the property investor or the property trader.

3   What This Guide is Not About

All of the tax strategies in this guide are legitimate ways of planning to minimise your tax liabilities.

In some cases, they involve "grey areas" of the tax legislation, where there is more than one way to interpret the law, and where this is the case, it is clearly indicated in the text.

This guide is not about complicated tax avoidance schemes, many of which do not work, or are vulnerable to retrospective legislation.

It is most emphatically not about ways to <u>evade</u> tax – that is, to reduce your tax bill dishonestly by telling the taxman less than the whole truth.

The above may seem obvious, but we mention it because we have sometimes been quite surprised by the advice taxpayers tell us they have received from other sources – in some cases, if they had followed that advice, they would have been straying over the line that separates (legal) tax avoidance from (criminal) tax evasion – a line that was famously described by Dennis Healey, the former Chancellor of the Exchequer, as having "the thickness of a prison wall!".

This distinction is so important that we will begin by looking at what separates tax planning, tax avoidance, and tax evasion.

4   Staying on the Right Side of the Prison Wall

"The thickness of a prison wall" – the difference between tax planning, tax avoidance, and tax evasion, and why it matters!

Taxation has rather murky origins – arguably, it began when a party of Norman soldiers rode into an English village, and stole all the chickens.

Perhaps one of the earliest examples of tax planning (or maybe tax avoidance, depending on your point of view) would have been hiding some of your chickens when you heard the approaching hoof beats.

As things got more sophisticated, both the way taxes were charged and the ways they were avoided became more complicated.

You can still see the bricked-up windows on old houses (done to avoid the 18th century Window Tax). It has been suggested that the first Lurchers (a delightful breed of dog: a cross between a greyhound and a pastoral breed such as a Border Collie) were bred to avoid the luxury tax on Greyhounds – in 1823, for example, the annual tax on a Greyhound was £1, whereas for any other breed of dog, it was only 8 shillings (40p).

If we fast forward to the present, the way the law now stands on trying to reduce your tax bill works like this:

4.1   Tax Planning and the Duke's Gardener

In 1935, the House of Lords gave their judgement in the case of the Duke of Westminster, who had set up a tax planning scheme involving his gardener (and other employees) and a Deed of Covenant – the details do not matter, as sadly that particular scheme no longer works.

Their lordships said the Duke's scheme successfully reduced his tax bill, and added that:

"Every man is entitled if he can to order his affairs so that the tax attaching under the appropriate Acts is less than it otherwise would be"

This remains true today, though there have been developments since that have chipped away at this principle.

4.2   Anti-avoidance Legislation

One of the reasons that the specific scheme used by the Duke of Westminster no longer works is that legislation was passed to prevent it from doing so in future.

For many years, this was the only way that the Government could counter tax avoidance schemes – by identifying how a specific scheme worked, and passing legislation to ensure it was no longer effective.

One of the problems with this approach (from HMRC's point of view) is that it is always a couple of years or so behind the times, and by the time the law is on the statute book, a way round it has been invented.

The other problem (from the taxpayer's point of view, this time) is that the anti-avoidance legislation can catch quite innocent transactions, or can apply in circumstances where the average taxpayer is simply unaware that the law exists, much less that it applies to him!

There are several examples of this type of legislation in this guide – to take two:

- The "Construction Industry Scheme" which requires property developers to deduct tax from certain payments to tradesmen, and keep records of payments to others

- Section 752 ITA 2007, which can turn what you thought was going to be a small capital gains tax bill into a large income tax bill

4.3   The "Ramsay" Doctrine

Since the early 1980s, the Courts have developed a new way of interpreting tax legislation (the name comes from one of the earliest cases on the subject, and has nothing to do with bad-tempered TV Chefs). The Ramsay doctrine says that:

If a tax planning scheme involves <u>a series of preordained steps</u>, and <u>one or more</u> of those steps has <u>no commercial purpose</u> except to <u>avoid tax</u>, then that step can be ignored, and you look at the <u>commercial reality</u> of the transaction rather than the form it has been given by the scheme.

This way of looking at the law came about as a result of a number of highly artificial and complex schemes to avoid tax that were being marketed at the time.

The Ramsay doctrine is still evolving, and it is something that cannot be ignored when considering tax planning ideas. In the course of this guide, you will find several examples where I warn that the Ramsay doctrine might be used by HMRC to attack a particular tax planning strategy, and how to minimise the risk of this happening.

4.4   The DOTAS Disclosure Rules

In the last few years, legislation has been passed that requires those who market certain types of complex tax avoidance schemes to disclose the details to HMRC.

Anyone who then uses one of these schemes has to disclose the fact in their tax return. There are severe penalties for failure to comply with these rules.

This requirement to disclose such schemes has two consequences for those who decide to use them:

- They can be sure that HMRC will look very closely at the scheme to see if it is technically effective, and if it is not, they will have the names of everyone who is using the scheme

- Even if the scheme works, it is likely that legislation (sometimes retrospective) will be introduced to block the scheme.

None of the tax planning strategies described in this guide falls into this dangerous category of tax planning scheme, and none of them requires to be disclosed to HMRC in this way.

4.5 Tax Evasion – The Other Side of the Prison Wall!

Tax planning and tax avoidance are both entirely legal. Tax evasion is a criminal offence. Tax evasion always involves dishonesty in some form or other.

For example:

- In the days of the window tax, some houses were built with "dummy" windows made of bricks, or the windows in existing houses were removed and bricked up – the tax only applied to glass windows. That was tax planning.

- In other cases, houses were designed with one very large window where previously there might have been two or more small ones.

  We have heard of a case where an entire course of bricks made of glass linked all the windows on one wall of a house, and it was claimed they were all one window for the purposes of the tax.

  The tax commissioners refused to accept this argument and the tax had to be paid. That was tax avoidance, though unsuccessful.

- Some people bricked up their windows only when the "Surveyor" from the Inland Revenue was due to inspect the property.

  There was no mortar holding the bricks in place, and they were removed after the Surveyor had gone, to reveal the glass window behind. That was tax evasion, and if you were caught doing it, your window tax was doubled!

Tax evasion is not confined to the "black economy" where payment is in cash and the taxman is never told about it.

It is likely that any "tax planning" scheme that relies on HMRC not knowing the full facts about a transaction is in fact an example of tax evasion.

Obviously, none of the strategies described in this guide involve tax evasion in any form, but in some cases (typically those involving tax planning for your home) we shall be pointing out the danger of crossing the line between avoidance and evasion.

4.6 GAAR

Since the 2013 Finance Act we have also had a "General Anti-Abuse Rule" or "GAAR".

Essentially, this enables HMRC to take action against artificial tax-planning schemes that seek to achieve results not intended by the tax legislation. It is most unlikely to have any effect on the sort of tax planning described in this book, if HMRC are to be believed, because they claim the GAAR is aimed exclusively at the sort of highly artificial tax schemes that would typically fall under the "Disclosure Rules" described in 4.4 above.

4.7 2014 Finance Act

This contained two other measures that took effect from Royal Assent to the Act in the summer of 2014:

- "Accelerated payment" will allow HMRC to serve notice on a taxpayer using a scheme disclosable under DOTAS (see above) or being countered by the GAAR, requiring them to pay the tax in dispute immediately rather than waiting for the result of the dispute with HMRC

- "Follower notices" can be issued by HMRC to those using avoidance schemes "similar" to any scheme HMRC win their case against in court. A "follower notice" requires the taxpayer using the "similar" scheme to amend their tax return to give up the tax saving from the avoidance scheme, or face a penalty.

These measures are again aimed at what HMRC might term "artificial" or "contrived" arrangements, such as might be found in "disclosable" schemes as above. We do not expect anything that we recommend in this book to fall foul of these measures, either.

5 Key Tax Dates for Your Diary

The UK's tax system is based on "Self-Assessment".

People who have untaxed income (such as rents from property or income from self-employment), or who have high incomes generally, are sent an annual Self-Assessment Return for each tax year, shortly after the end of that year on 5 April.

If you are in this category, you will already be familiar with the way the system works, and the relevant deadlines for filing your return and paying the tax.

If you do not receive a self-assessment return each April, however, and you either:

- Start receiving untaxed income, such as rental income from property, or

- Make a capital gain which is not exempt from CGT

It is your responsibility to notify HMRC and to request a Self-Assessment Return.

The deadline for this is 5 October after the end of the tax year, so if you first let a property during the year ending 5 April 2014, you must notify HMRC of this by 5 October 2014. The deadline for a new self-employed **trader** (such as a property developer) is shorter, and is dealt with later in this guide.

Once in the "self-assessment" system, you are required to file the return (by 31 October after the end of the tax year if you file a paper return, and 31 January if you do it online) and pay any tax due by 31 January following the end of the tax year – so for 2016/17, the tax (and the return if filed online) will be due on 31 January 2018.

In future years, you will be required to make annual payments on account, on 31 July and on 31 January – your Self-Assessment Return will explain the details.

There are penalties for failing to notify HMRC of your new source of income, or your capital gains, by the 5 October deadline, so do not delay!

In the Chancellor's pre-election Budget in March 2015 it was announced that there would be radical changes to the system described above, with more reliance on frequent online contact between HMRC and the taxpayer. At the time of writing it is not clear exactly how these changes will affect the self-assessment process, although the Chancellor seems to think that making quarterly online returns will somehow be less troublesome than a single annual return. We, and seemingly the majority of advisers, remain to be convinced.

6 Anti-Avoidance Legislation - Chapter 3 Part 13 of ITA 2007

We shall shortly be looking at the taxation of property developers, but before we do, we need to consider this piece of anti-avoidance legislation, which can cause problems for the owners of investment properties or other land when they sell it – not least because many people have never heard of it!

Section 752 introduces Chapter 3 of Part 13 of the Income Tax Act 2007. The first words of section 752 are:

"This Chapter has effect for the purpose of preventing the avoidance of income tax by persons concerned with land or the development of land"

What the section does is to treat certain transactions in land as if they produced income rather than capital gains- and this can be expensive!

Case Study - 1   "A slice of the action" and "Chapter 3"

Norman has owned three buy to let properties since March 1999 – they cost him a total of £100,000.

He is thinking of selling them, and has had a valuation of £450,000 for the three properties from an estate agent.

In 2016, he is approached by a developer, who is confident he can get planning permission to build a shopping complex on Norman's land.

He offers Norman a deal:

- £400,000 up front when Norman sells him the properties

- £50,000 when he gets full planning permission for the development

- A "slice of the action", in the form of 20% of the profit on the development itself (the developer reckons Norman's 20% could be worth up to £200,000)

This "slice of the action" will be payable one year after the initial payment.

Norman accepts the deal.

He knows a bit about capital gains tax, including the way "contingent consideration" (the payment on getting planning permission) and "unascertainable future consideration" (the "slice of the action") are taxed, and so he *expects* that he will be taxed as follows:

"The £400,000 and the £50,000, together with the present value of the future right to up to £200,000 will be added together, and treated as the sale price – if I assume that the present value of the 20% "slice of the action" is agreed as £150,000, the total sale price will be £600,000. With a base cost of £100,000, I will make a gain of £500,000, taxable at 28%."

(Norman also figures that, if he eventually gets more than the £150,000 that his "slice of the action" was valued at, he will also pay CGT on that amount, again at 28%).

Unfortunately, Norman will be caught by the Chapter 3 rules, because his "slice of the action" is actually giving him a chance to participate in the profits of a trading transaction (the development and sale of the shopping complex), and this is therefore taxable as income, rather than as a capital gain.

Note while the Chancellor recently announced in the March 2016 Budget that CGT rates will generally fall to 10% and 20% (for higher rate taxpayers), the higher rates of 18% and 28% will remain for residential property gains – and in this context, the latest guidance says that this will include "…land that has, at any time in the person's ownership, consisted of or included a dwelling", so Norman will be caught.

Although the initial £450,000 will still be taxed as a capital gain, anything Norman gets under his "slice of the action" of the developer's profit on sale, will be taxed as income under the Chapter 3 rules.

Let us assume that Norman's "slice of the action" actually produces the £200,000 the developer had predicted, and that Norman is already a higher rate taxpayer, so all taxable gains will be at 28%.

Treated as all capital gain:

Gain on initial payment (600K-100K)	500,000	Tax payable
Less Annual Exempt Amount	(11,100)	
Taxable	488,900	
CGT @ 28%	136,892	136,892
Gain in later tax year on "Slice of the action" 200,000, less 150,000 already taxed above	50,000	
Annual exempt amount (say)	(11,100)	
Taxable	38,900	
CGT @ 28%	10,892	10,892
Total CGT due		**147,784**

Because of the Chapter 3 rules, the treatment is very different:

Gain on initial payment (450K-100K)	350,000	Tax payable
Less Annual Exempt Amount	(11,100)	
Taxable	338,900	
CGT @ 28%	94,892	94,892
"Slice of the action" treated as income in 2017/18	200,000	
Income tax @ 40/45% (say)	85,000	85,000
Total tax due		**179,892**

> **Caution:** Chapter 3 is very complicated, and we have simplified the way it works for the purposes of this Case Study, which is intended simply to illustrate the sort of circumstances that can be caught.

Now the good news:

- Chapter 3 rules cannot apply to a gain on the disposal of a main residence, even if it is caught by the "intention to realise a gain" rules – see 8.11 below.

  Mr Green, in 8.3 below, might have a problem, however, if he were given a "slice of the action" on the sale of part of his garden, because as we shall see, that did not qualify for the main residence exemption.

- In a case where you are not certain if you will be caught by the Chapter 3 rules, it is possible to get a "clearance" from HMRC before you agree to the deal.

  Provided you give them the full facts, if they then agree not to apply the Chapter 3 rules, they cannot change their minds later.

"Slice of the action" deals are not the only type of transaction that can be caught by the Chapter 3 rules, but they are by far the commonest example of how people can be caught by the section without either realising it, or having intended to avoid tax.

"Chapter 3" is definitely a job for a tax expert, and you should consult your tax adviser about it if:

- You are offered a "slice of the action" deal for the sale of land, or

- You are offered any deal involving the sale of land that seems rather complicated

7   Trading in Property

If you buy a property with the intention of selling it on at a profit in the short term, then even if you receive some rental income from it while you own it, you are **trading** and your profit from selling the property will be charged to income tax – and to National Insurance Contributions.

In this section of the guide, we shall look at the tax treatment of:

- "Turnarounds" where a property is bought (perhaps at an auction) and sold at a profit with little or no work done on it

- "Refurbs" where a property is bought, significantly altered (perhaps by being converted into flats, or by being extensively renovated), and then sold at a profit

- "New builds", where a new property is built and sold.

7.1   Notifying HMRC you have started trading

Notification:
When you begin to trade, you must notify HMRC immediately. If you do not do so, you may be charged to interest on any Class 2 NIC paid late, and there are potentially quite severe penalties for longer delays.

The simplest way to register is to visit the "Self-Assessment" page on HMRC's website. (Strictly now the GOV.UK website, although much yet remains on the old HMRC domain).

7.2   National Insurance (NI) Contributions

A trader is liable to pay "Class 4" NIC on his profits.

2016/17 NI Rates	
First £8,060	NIL
Next £34,940	9%
Any additional profits	2%

In addition to Class 4 NIC, you are also usually required to pay "Class 2" NIC, calculated at a rate of £2.80 per week and recently amended so that, by default, it will be collected alongside Class 4 NIC and income tax on your self-assessment return.

Class 2 NIC is to be abolished from April 2018 and Class 4 NIC will effectively take over as the contributory element that secures eligibility for state pension.

If you ring the Newly Self-Employed Helpline, (0300 200 3504), you should be sent full details of all of this, and how to set up your direct debit or other ways to pay.

If you are also an employee, it may be possible to reduce your Class 4 NIC (but not the Class 2), for example if you are already paying the maximum employee NI contributions through PAYE on your salary.

7.3   Income Tax and NIC for the Property Developer

The following Case Study illustrates how income tax and NIC are charged on a property developer's profits:

Case Study - 2	Charging of Income Tax and NIC

Simon sets himself up as a property developer, buying a rundown house on 6 April 2016 for £70,000. He spends £30,000 on renovation work, and sells the house on 1st March 2017 for £150,000.

He has made a profit of £50,000. Assuming he has no other income for 2013/14, his profit will be taxed as follows:

Income Tax		Payable
Profit for 2016/17	50,000	
Less personal allowance	(11,000)	Nil
Taxed at 20%	(32,000)	6,400
Balance taxed at 40%	7,000	2,800
National Insurance Class 4	50,000	
First 8,060	(8,060)	Nil
8,061 – 43,000 at 9%	(34,940)	3,145
Balance at 2%	7,000	140
Total tax and NIC payable 31 January 2017		12,485
Plus Class 2 NIC payable		146

7.4   Property Development and Limited Companies

In some cases, it may be advantageous to use a limited company for your property development trade. This is because a company pays corporation tax at only 20% on its profits – so on a profit of £50,000 like Simon's, the corporation tax would be only £10,000.

The situation is not as simple as this, however – if you want to extract the cash from the company there will be additional tax costs. The decision whether to use a company or not is not an easy one – see our guide "**Dos and Don'ts for Property Tax Companies**", available from www.property-tax-portal.co.uk.

7.5   Accounts and Records

It is essential to set up a good record keeping system to keep track of your income and outgoings, and to keep those records safely – this is equally true of rental income, of course, but in the case of trading records, you are required to keep the records until the fifth anniversary of the 31 January after the end of the tax year – so for 2016/17, the records must be kept until at least 31 January 2023.

A trader's accounts must be prepared on the "accruals" basis – See 10.4 – but unlike a property investor, you may make up your accounts to any date you wish.

For each tax year, you will be taxed on the profits of the accounting year ending during that tax year – if your accounts are made up to the year ending 30 September, for example, for the tax year 2016/17 you will pay tax on your profits for the year ending 30 September 2016.

In the first couple of years of trading, the method is slightly different:

- First year – you will be taxed on the profits from the date you began trading to the following 5 April – so if you started trading on 1 October 2015, you would be taxed on the profits from 1 October 2015 to 5 April 2016 for 2015/16.

  If you make your accounts up to a different date, the profits will be apportioned to arrive at the correct figure for the period to 5 April.

- Second year – Basically the profits of your first twelve months of trading

> The fine detail of how profits in the early years are taxed, and the choice of the most tax-efficient accounting date, can be very complicated, and you would be wise to seek advice from your accountant or tax adviser.

7.6   The Construction Industry Scheme ("CIS")

If you engage in "property development", you will be required to register for and operate this scheme.

It does not normally apply to property investors (such as Buy To Let landlords), and if you really only do minimal refurbishment on your "turnarounds" you MAY be able to justify not joining it, but if you do "refurbs", or if you engage in property development,

you will be a "property developer" for the purposes of the CIS, and you must register as a "contractor".

What do these words mean?

A "property developer" could be an individual, a partnership, or a limited company. The key is, do they earn their profits by doing building work – either by new builds which they then sell, or by buying an existing property and improving it and selling it on? If so, then they are a property developer.

A **"contractor"** is someone whose business involves using other people's labour to carry out building work. Almost all "property developers" use the services of independent bricklayers, carpenters, painters, electricians, plasterers, and so on, so almost all of them will be "contractors".

A "Buy to let" investor will probably **not** be a "property developer" or "contractor" because, although he may use the same tradesmen to do work on his properties, he makes his income from renting them out, not from selling them – he is an investor, not a trader. If he spends more than £1million per year on "construction operations", however, he will be in the scheme as a "deemed contractor". Likewise, if he undertakes a substantial development project – even for letting purposes – HMRC may argue that he is temporarily "caught" by the regime.

The "Construction Industry Scheme" imposes very onerous duties on "contractors" and "subcontractors". In order to understand why the scheme is as it is, we need to look at its history.

Back in the 1960s, the construction industry in the UK was notorious for widespread tax evasion. Workers on building sites, who told the foreman their names were "Michael Mouse", or "Roy Rogers", got paid in cash, and had never seen a tax return in their lives. When the taxman attempted to trace them, to his surprise there was no Mr Mouse at the given address – and often the address was false as well.

There were two basic problems:

- Some of the "Mickey Mice" were really employees of the building contractor, and should have had PAYE applied to their wages

- The rest of them, though genuinely self-employed, did not declare their income and pay tax on it as they should have done

Against this background, the "Construction Industry Scheme" ("**CIS**") was first introduced in 1970. Since then, it has been much modified – with a major "reform" in 1999, and more major changes taking place in April 2007. The basic concept of the scheme remains the same, however.

The CIS is based on HMRC's distrust of everyone involved in the construction industry. It assumes that if builders are allowed to conduct their tax affairs like any other business in the land, they will lie and cheat and not pay their tax.

Jack owns a plot of land with planning permission to build a house on it. He decides he will build a house and sell it.

At this point, Jack has decided to trade as a property developer – a speculative builder, in fact – so he is now a "contractor" for CIS purposes. Jack must immediately register with HMRC as a "contractor". He is obliged to read through many pages of guidance on how to operate the scheme as an unpaid tax collector.

Jack talks to Bob (the builder), and they agree a price for Bob and his men to build the house. It is agreed that Jack will pay Bob £5,000 when his men start work.

Jack must contact HMRC (by phone or online) to verify if Bob is registered as a subcontractor.

Jack eventually gets through to HMRC, who confirm Bob is registered for "Gross Payment".

Jack can pay Bob without deducting tax.

Jack has also asked an electrician, Michael Faraday, to do the wiring on the new house. Before paying him, he contacts HMRC, who tell him Michael is registered for "Net Payment".

Jack must deduct 20% tax from payments to Michael. If Michael had not been registered at all, the tax to deduct would have been 30%.

Once a month, Jack must send the tax he has deducted to HMRC, together with a return of payments made, signed to certify that he has operated the scheme correctly. This must be done within 14 days of the end of the month (but Jack must remember that a CIS month ends of the 5th day of the following month, so in fact he has until 19 July to send in his deductions for June).

That was a VERY abbreviated version of how the scheme works – the reality is more complicated and difficult to comply with.

7.7   Why Bother with the CIS?

The short answer is that there are penalties if you don't!

If Jack failed to register as a contractor, or failed to deduct tax from payments to Michael, he could be liable for:

- Penalties of up to £900 for **each** late monthly return he makes (it could be more in cases where the CIS tax is high enough – and an extra £3,000 or more per return if HMRC decides the failure was deliberate)

- Unless Jack can satisfy HMRC that Michael has paid his tax himself, the 20% tax that Jack should have deducted from the payments he made to Michael

If you are trading as a property developer, building (or buying and improving) properties for sale, you are a "Contractor" and liable to operate the CIS. There is no lower limit below which you do not have to operate this scheme.

One of the many unjust features of the CIS regime is that there are probably a lot of small scale property developers out there who do not know they should be operating the scheme.

Those who comply with the scheme are at a disadvantage, because many small "domestic" building firms will simply not work for a CIS "contractor" because of the bureaucratic and cashflow implications; builders who work only on people's own homes are not required to be in the CIS.

To find out more about the CIS, visit HMRC's website and look for "CIS".

7.8   VAT

This is unlikely to be an issue for the typical buy to let landlord, as the letting of residential property is an exempt supply, so he cannot claim back any of the input tax on his expenses. For the "turnaround" or the "refurb", the purchase and sale of an existing property is **usually** an exempt supply as well, so again it will not be possible to recover the VAT.

But it is possible still to reduce your VAT costs – for example, if a property has been vacant for over two years, or if you buy it and then change the number of dwellings it contains (for example by converting it into flats, or by knocking two flats into one), then although the *sale* of the building may still be exempt, any VAT registered contractor you use may be able to charge you a reduced rate of 5% VAT on their invoices, including the cost of most materials (the normal rate of VAT is currently 20%).

A commercial property landlord may decide to register for VAT so that he can recover the VAT on his expenses. If he wants to do this, he will have to "opt to tax" the rents he charges. Whether he decides to do this or not will depend on the sort of tenants he has – if they are themselves fully taxable for VAT purposes (as most businesses are), they will be quite happy, as they will be able to recover the VAT on the rent.

If, on the other hand, the tenants are 'small' traders who are below the threshold for VAT registration and do not want to register voluntarily, or if they are exempt or partially exempt (as are most financial businesses and insurance companies), they will be very unenthusiastic about paying VAT on the rent which they cannot recover.

A property developer doing only new residential builds may well want to register for VAT, because when he sells the completed building, it will be "zero rated" so he will be able to recover his VAT without having to charge VAT to the purchaser.

Typically, the problems arise when the business engages in a mixture of these activities – for example, if it does new builds and refurbs, then some of its sales will be exempt from VAT (i.e., most refurbs), and some will be zero rated (sales of new builds). This will mean that the business is "partially exempt", which in turn can lead to problems in recovering the VAT on costs that cannot be specifically attributed to specific sales (such as, dare I say it, fees from the business' Tax Adviser!).

The above is a very brief summary of the main VAT issues that may arise for a trader involved with property.

> Caution: **The VAT treatment of land and buildings is one of the most complicated aspects of VAT.** If you are planning to engage in property development or refurbishment/conversions to let out, you should take advice from a suitably qualified Tax Adviser.

7.9   Property Developers and Trading Stock

As a trader in property, the land or properties you buy for resale are your **trading stock.** At the end of each year, you include the cost of any stock you have not sold in your balance sheet, and it becomes your "opening stock" for your next year of trading. This means that you do not get a tax deduction for your trading stock until you sell it:

Case Study - 4   Trading Stock

Letitia begins trading as a property developer. In her first year she buys two plots of land, Plot A and Plot B, for £10,000 each.

At the end of the year, she has spent £40,000 on constructing a house on Plot A, and £30,000 on constructing a house on Plot B. She has not sold either house.

Her "Closing Stock" for Year 1 will be:

- Plot A £50,000
- Plot B £40,000
- Total £90,000

During Year 2, she spends another £10,000 on Plot A, finishing the house, which she sells for £100,000. She spends another £30,000 on Plot B, but does not sell it.

For Year 2, her stock will be:

- Opening Stock (from Year 1)   £90,000
- Add Expenditure in year   £40,000
- Deduct Cost of Stock sold (Plot A)   (£60,000)
- Closing stock (Plot B)   £70,000

The £60,000 expenditure on Plot A is deducted from the £100,000 sale proceeds to arrive at the profit on that sale. Note that closing stock equates to the cost to date in Plot B.

This is a simplified version of how trading stock works, but the important point is that the cost of your stock is carried forward until you sell it. If you are considering substantial property development projects – and particularly those that may take several accounting periods to complete – you should take expert advice on how closing stock, work-in-progress and "long term contracts" are valued.

7.10   Property Not Acquired as Trading Stock

In most cases, it will be clear that a property developer is trading – he buys bare land or a building, builds on the land or improves the building, and then sells it.

The situation is not so clear cut if the land or building was not acquired as trading stock, such as where it is inherited, or where a buy to let investor decides to develop and sell a property he has owned and rented out for some time.

Case Study - 5   Land Not Acquired as Trading Stock

Rebecca inherited a two-acre field from her aunt in 2001. It was valued at £7,000, as at the time there was no prospect of getting planning permission for it.

She used the field to graze her horse until 2013, when it became apparent that it might now be possible to get planning permission for four houses.

- If Rebecca simply gets outline planning permission and sells the land, she will realise a capital gain.

- If she sells the land to a developer on a "slice of the action" deal, she will make a capital gain, though she may have problems with section 752 – see Case Study - 1.

- If she decides to do the development herself, hiring architects, builders, and so on to construct the houses, and sells them, the position is more complicated.

  The most likely interpretation of the facts will be that at the point that she decided to go ahead with the development, she "appropriated" the land as trading stock.

If you "appropriate" a capital asset you own to trading stock, you are treated as if you had disposed of it for CGT purposes at its market value, and in your trading accounts you treat it as if you had bought it at the same value.

If you wish, you can elect to "hold over" the capital gain you make on the land by "appropriating" it, so that you do not pay CGT, but the whole profit (including held over gain) is taxed as a profit of your trade when you sell it. It may be to your advantage **not** to do this, however, as CGT is charged at up to 28%, (for residential property), whereas your trading profits will be taxed at up to 45%, plus NIC.

Rebecca's brother Tom inherited a rundown old house from another aunt. He decided to sell it immediately, but first he spent some money on extensively refurbishing and improving it.

Whether Tom is trading or not is a more difficult question – he is not changing the nature of the asset he inherited (a house) but merely taking steps to get the best price for it.

If he wanted to, he could almost certainly win the argument that his sale of the house produced a capital gain (and the cost of the improvements would be allowable as a deduction from that gain).

Alternatively, however, he could formally "appropriate" the house to a new trade of property development.

Why would he want to do this? If he stuck with the capital gains route, he would have his annual exempt amount of £11,100 to deduct from the gain, whereas if he becomes a trader he will be liable to income tax on the profit, AND to NIC – at potentially a much higher overall rate.

There are two reasons why he might make the choice to trade:

- Certainty – the whole issue of when you start trading with property like this is a "grey area", but if you "appropriate" the asset to trading stock, HMRC will find it very difficult to argue that you have not done this.

- Interest on loans – if Tom had to borrow money to pay for the improvements, he would not get relief for the interest he paid if the property were sold for a capital gain, whereas for a property developer, the interest would be allowable as a deduction from trading profits

There is a third possible reason for this "appropriation" – it is sometimes better to trade as a property developer through a limited company, and "appropriating" an asset to trading stock can be the first stage in transferring it into a limited company.

7.11   Taking Out Trading Stock for Your Own Use

In a way, this is the reverse of the previous Case Study. If you are trading as a property developer, and you decide you would like to keep one of the houses in your trading stock (either to live in it yourself, or to let it out for the long term), you will come up against the notoriously unfair rule derived from the tax case of **Sharkey v Wernher.** So notoriously unfair, in fact, that it was at risk of serious challenge until it was turned into legislation – ITTOIA 2005 ss172A – F. I recall a very competent tax barrister offering to take cases *pro bono*, and HMRC simply refused to hear them before tribunal – probably because they feared they might lose. Instead, they changed the law, arguably to spare HMRC's blushes.

If you are a property developer, therefore, and you decide to keep one of your houses for yourself, whether to live in or to let out, your business will be taxed as if it had sold that house to you at its market value.

The moral of this is to make your mind up quickly – before you build the house - so that you can take the **land** out of the business at its (presumably much lower) market value, and then all you have to do is disallow the cost of building your house.

7.12   Expenses for Property Developers

It is important to understand the distinction between Capital and Revenue, both for receipts and for expenses.

There have been numerous tax cases on this issue, and the distinction can be very fine in the "grey areas" between the two, but as far as the typical property letting business is concerned, the path is quite well-trodden, and there are some clear distinctions to be made.

Capital expenditure involves acquiring an "enduring asset" for your business – the most obvious example being buying a property that you intend to keep and use as the HQ of your development business.

A **Capital receipt** involves receiving a payment for disposing of such an asset – again, the most obvious example would be selling a property that you have been using as your HQ.

Revenue expenditure means expenses that do not produce an "enduring asset" – the basic running costs of your business. An obvious example would be travelling expenses.

Revenue receipts mean the income produced from the business – such as the sale of the developed properties.

You deduct **revenue expenses** from **revenue receipts** to arrive at your **profit** for **income tax** purposes.

You deduct **capital expenditure** from **capital receipts** to arrive at the **capital gains** you make from disposing of your "fixed assets".

As we shall see, there can sometimes be problems in deciding exactly where the line should be drawn between capital and revenue, particularly where expenditure is concerned.

7.13   "Wholly and Exclusively"

In order to be allowable as an expense, expenditure must have been incurred "wholly and exclusively" for the purposes of the business.

In some cases, expenses are incurred partly for the purposes of the business, and partly for other purposes.

Provided that it is possible to arrive at an objective way of apportioning the expense between business and private elements, the business part can be claimed as an expense. For example, you may use your car partly for the purpose of your business (visiting properties, etc.), and partly for private purposes.

If you keep a record of your business and private mileage, you can claim the business proportion of the running costs of the car.

There are some cases where it is impossible to say that any proportion of an expense was incurred "wholly and exclusively" for the purpose of the business, even though the business was one of the reasons for the expenditure.

The classic example is clothing. Although clothing that has a specific protective function, such as safety helmets and overalls, is an allowable expense, ordinary clothing is not.

Even if, for example, you buy cheap jeans specifically to wear on site visits, they are not allowable as an expense because they can be regarded as normal everyday clothing that serves a private purpose of keeping you warm, etc.

7.14   Allowable Expenses

Subject to the rules on capital expenditure and the "wholly and exclusively" rule, pretty much all of the expenses you incur in order to earn the profits of your property development business can be deducted to arrive at your profit.

Particular care is needed with certain types of expenditure:

- Wages and salaries for spouse or children – while it can be a tax efficient idea to employ your family in the business (because if they have no other income, they can use their personal allowance and lower rate bands against their wages), you must be able to justify the amounts you pay them as being reasonable commercial pay for the work they do – "wholly and exclusively", again.

- Business Entertaining is not an allowable expense. One exception is annual staff parties – these are an allowable expense, (and tax-free for the employees, provided the cost per head is not more than £150 for the year).

- Accountancy fees for preparing your accounts are allowable expenses. Strictly speaking, the costs of agreeing your tax liabilities are not (because they are not "wholly and exclusively" incurred to earn the profits, but rather to measure the tax once the profits have been earned).

  There is, however, a long-standing practice of allowing the costs of normal tax compliance fees.

- Training costs for your employees are generally allowable, provided there is some business benefit to the training.

  The costs of your training as the owner of the business are more problematic. If the training is merely to update you, then the cost will be allowable.

  If the training teaches you new skills, and particularly if it results in a recognised qualification, then HMRC will argue that it is a capital expense (because your new skills/qualifications are an asset of enduring benefit to the business) and as such not allowable.

  For example, I regularly attend training courses to keep myself up to date with the latest developments in tax, and these are an allowable expense for me.

  I am also qualified as a Chartered Tax Adviser, which involved several training courses and examinations. If I had incurred this expenditure myself as a sole trader or a partner, it would not have been allowable, but fortunately for me, it was paid for by my employers at the time. They will have got a deduction for the cost, because it was for training an employee.

- Travelling expenses – these deserve a section to themselves:

7.15   Travelling Expenses

If you travel "wholly and exclusively" for the purposes of your property development business, you can deduct the costs of that travel.

It is important to determine where your business is run from.

If you keep all of the paperwork at home and use your home as the office for the business, then travel from your home to any of your properties or development sites, or to another business venue (a DIY store for materials, for example) will be an allowable expense. HMRC will, however, challenge this unless you can show that your home is genuinely the place where you carry on your business. If you use a letting agent, for example, they will argue that it is his office, not your home that is your place of business.

If you have an office away from your home where you run the business, then travel from your home to that office will not be allowable, but travel from that office to business destinations will be.

The other pitfall is "duality of purpose". If there is a substantial private benefit from your journey, HMRC will say part of its purpose was not for business, and again disallow the expenditure:

Case Study - 6   Duality of Purpose

Max lives outside Birmingham, and is engaged on a renovation in the city. He travels from home to the site, spends ten minutes discussing progress with the foreman, and then parks near the Bullring and does his weekly shopping before returning home.

Because the journey had a substantial private purpose, he cannot claim a deduction for it.

The following week, he makes the same trip to see the foreman, but this time the only other shopping he does is to stop at a garage to fill up with petrol and buy a newspaper and a packet of cigarettes. In this case, the private benefit of the journey is clearly trivial, and so he can deduct the cost.

The cost of a journey in your car is the proportionate cost of running the car for the year, so you will need to keep a record of:

- Business and private mileage (keep a notebook in the car, and record the business mileage. If you also make a note of the total mileage as at 6 April and the following 5 April, you will be able to work out your business/private proportion). If you are a trader and make up your accounts to a different date and not to 5 April, record the total mileage each year at that date.

- Cost of petrol, oil, screenwash, etc. **Keep the receipts.**

- Cost of insurance, MOT, Road Tax, AA/RAC membership

- Cost of interest on loan used to buy car (not repayments of capital)

- Cost of servicing and repairs. **Keep the receipts**

You can then claim the business proportion of the above costs, together with all costs incurred directly on a business journey, such as parking and tolls.

7.16   Cost of Car and Capital Allowances

You can claim capital allowances on the cost of your car, again based on the business proportion.

The rules for expenditure on cars incurred after April 2009 have changed, and they are now simply claimed at one of the two "rates" for capital allowances – the 8% rate if their CO_2 emissions are over 130 g/km, or the 18% rate if their emissions are equal to or under 130 g/km.

Case Study - 7   Capital Allowances on Car

Max's proportion of business to private mileage for the year is 10% Business to 90% private. He buys a car (emissions under 130 g/km) on 6 April 2015, for £16,000. For 2016/17, his capital allowances on the car are worked out as follows:

2015/16		Private (90%)	Business (10%)	Deduction Allowed
Cost of car	16,000			2015/16
WDA 18%	(2,880)	2,592	288	288
2016/17				2016/17
Cost brought forward	13,120			
WDA 18%	2,362	2,126	236	236
Cost carried forward to 2017/18	10,758			

In 2017/18, Max sells the car for £11,000:

2017/18		Private (90%)	Business (10%)	Balancing charge added to profits
Cost brought forward	10,758			2017/18
Sale proceeds	11,000			
Balancing charge	242	218	24	24

Note this assumes Max's business/private proportion remains the same each year – in practice it is likely it would vary from year to year, and the balancing charge (or balancing allowance if Max sold the car for less than its brought forward cost) would be based on the average for the period he had owned the car. Note also that the rules for employees' cars are a little different.

7.17 Alternative Method for Car Mileage

Sole traders and partners (and company directors or employees using their own car for business) are allowed to avoid all this complexity by using a standard figure per **business** mile to claim their car mileage costs. For 2015/16, the rate is:

First 10,000 business miles in tax tear = 45p per mile
Subsequent business miles in tax year = 25p per mile

Note - you cannot switch between the strict method and the 45p/25p method – once you adopt one method for a particular car, you must stay with it until you change the car.

7.18 Other Capital Allowances

As a trader, you can also claim Capital Allowances on other "Plant and Machinery" you buy for the purposes of your business, such as:

- Office equipment

- Vans, lorries, etc.

- Machinery such as cement mixers, compressors, etc.

- Computers, fax machines, etc.

The basic principle is that you claim an "annual investment allowance" of 100% ("AIA") on the first £200,000 (from January 2016) you spend for the year. The remaining expenditure is the subject of a "Writing Down Allowance" of 18% each year thereafter on any balance left over:

The AIA does not apply to cars, hence the drawn-out calculations above. Certain assets with exceptionally long lives or that are "integral" to buildings get writing down allowances of only 8%. They do however qualify for inclusion in the AIA of £200,000.

7.19 Employed or Self Employed?

As part of your property development business, you will almost certainly have other people working for you.

If they are involved in "construction operations", you will already have considered the Construction Industry Scheme (CIS – see paragraph 7.6), but there is another important distinction to consider.

> **Caution:** Note that the first thing to consider for a new worker is not the CIS – this will only apply once you have satisfied yourself that the worker concerned is self-employed and **not** an employee.

Anyone who does work for your business may be either self-employed (as you will be yourself, unless you use a company for your business), or they may be employed by you. If they are an employee then you are required to operate the PAYE system to collect tax and NIC from their wages.

Problems often arise where a person assures you he is "self-employed" when in fact he should be treated by you as an employee.

Even if he is genuinely self-employed in another capacity, he may be employed by you because of the terms under which he works for you.

The distinction between employment and self-employment can be very difficult to make. Some basic questions to ask yourself are:

- Is this person genuinely in business on his own account – is he able to make extra profit by doing the job efficiently, or at risk of losing money if he is inefficient?

- Does he provide his own equipment and materials?

- Does he agree a price for a job, or does he charge by the hour?

- Does he get holiday pay or sick pay?

- Does he have to do the work personally, or can he send one of his own employees to do it for him? If he can, he is not your employee.

- Does he do a specific job for which you agree terms, or is he just available for you to use for any reasonable task?

- If he makes a mess of a job, or damages something, is he liable to make it good at his own time/expense?

- Does he do the work on his own terms (for example, you agree a deadline, but then how he meets that deadline is up to him), or does he work as and when you tell him to do so?

None of these is conclusive, except perhaps for the "substitution" test at the fifth bullet point above, but together they will build up a picture of the relationship and help to decide if it is one of employment or self-employment.

If you have any doubts as to whether someone working for you is employed or self-employed, it is important to take advice from a tax adviser. This is because if you get it wrong, you may incur significant extra tax liabilities:

7.20   Grossing Up

Where someone wrongly treated as self-employed has received payments that should have been made under PAYE, the inspector will generally argue that the tax liability should be settled by the employer rather than the employee, and that this should be done by "grossing up" the payments made.

Case Study - 8   Grossing Up

Bob has been working for you as a driver and general assistant, and has been paid without deduction of PAYE because you both wrongly thought he was self-employed. He has been paid £250 per week. It is agreed that this should have been paid under PAYE.

Bob has full tax allowances, so for him to have received £250 in cash, the PAYE deductions would have been:

Gross payment	277
Less income tax at 20%	(13)
Less employee's NIC at 12%	(14)
Gives weekly cash	250

In addition, the company would have had to pay employers NIC at 13.8% on the £277 – another £16. So, because you paid Bob without operating PAYE, the annual amount of tax and NIC the inspector will seek to claim will be:

Weekly income tax	13
Weekly employee NIC	14
Weekly employer's NIC	16
Weekly total	43
Times 52 gives	2,236

(Note – the PAYE year is often 53 weeks long, and also note it is HMRC practice to round down to the nearest pound!)

"Grossing up" does not always happen – but it is almost always the position HMRC start from, and you will need a Tax Adviser who has experience of negotiating with HMRC on these cases to ensure the damage is limited as much as possible. The other good news is that, provided Bob has paid his self-employed income tax and NIC, the amounts he has paid can usually be deducted from the tax and NIC shown above.

7.21   Losses

Because property development is a trade, if you make a loss in any tax year, you can set this loss against any other income you may have for that year (salary, investment income, pension, and so on), and claim a tax repayment. In the case of losses at the beginning or end of your trading enterprise, the loss can be carried back to earlier years.

The detailed calculation of a loss for tax purposes, and how to set it off against other income, can be extremely complicated – take professional advice if you are in this situation.

7.22   Finance

The basic proposition is a simple one – any interest on loans taken out "wholly and exclusively" for the purpose of financing the business is an allowable expense, as are the costs of getting those loans – arrangement fees, valuations, guarantee fees, and so on.

This applies whatever the kind of loan involved – a mortgage, a bank loan, and even an overdraft, provided it is an overdraft on an account used solely for the business.

In order to understand the concept of "wholly and exclusively" as it applies to loan interest, we need to look at "the proprietor's capital account".

7.23   Proprietor's Capital Account

The proprietor's capital account is a record of the proprietor's financial relationship with his business.

On the plus side, it will have any "capital introduced" into the business – such as if, when you first decide to trade as a property developer, you buy a development property for cash, using your own savings; or if, later on, you pay for business expenses out of your private resources. To this will be added the profits made each year – but if the business makes losses, these will be deducted.

On the other side, your "drawings" will be deducted – these are the sums of money you take out of the business for your own use, for private expenditure, to pay your taxes, and so on.

As long as the proprietor's capital account is not overdrawn, any interest paid by the business on loans for business purposes is an allowable expense. If it becomes overdrawn, then some of the interest may be disallowed.

Karen sets up in business as a property developer. She buys a rundown property for £40,000, using her life savings. After spending £30,000 on renovating it (financed by an overdraft) she sells it for £110,000, thus making a profit of £40,000. For the first year, her capital account looks like this:

Capital introduced	40,000
Add profit for year	40,000
Total	80,000
Deduct drawings:	
Income tax/NIC (say 40%)	(16,000)
Cash taken for private use	(20,000)
Balance on capital account	44,000

(Note that the example assumes that the business account will pay Karen's tax bill, etc., and roughly £400 per week in personal expenses).

The capital account is not overdrawn, so all of the interest paid on the overdraft is an allowable expense.

Even if Karen had decided to treat herself to some expensive luxuries, she could have spent up to another £44,000 (financed from the business overdraft if she wanted) and all the interest would still be allowable.

Karen continues trading for some years, financing the business via the overdraft

She has a couple of bad years where she makes losses, but as the business is now her only source of income, she still has to draw cash for her living expenses.

In year 3, her capital account looks like this:

Balance from previous year	30,000
Deduct loss for year	(20,000)
Total	10,000
Deduct drawings:	
Income tax/NIC (nil – losses)	NIL

Cash for private use	(20,000)
Capital account overdrawn	(10,000)

Because Karen's capital account is overdrawn, HMRC will argue that part of the overdraft interest is being used to finance her drawings of £20,000, and is therefore not allowable as a deduction against profits.

This is a simplified calculation: the exact amount of the interest that will be disallowed is quite complex and adjustments are required for things like losses and depreciation, but the principle should be clear – if your drawings are greater than the money you put into the business at the start plus the profits you have made, then HMRC will argue that some of the loans are financing your drawings and not the business. The rules for interest in companies are quite different.

7.24   Loans for Mixed Purposes

Where possible, it is best to avoid using loans on accounts that are mainly used for private purposes, as these can lead to complications.

For example, if you use your private credit card to pay for business expenses, you can treat those expenses as part of the "capital introduced" into the business, as described above. If you want to claim a deduction for the interest on the credit card, however, you would need to treat the whole of the credit card account as part of your capital account with the business, in order to differentiate the business and private elements.

This is possible in theory, but potentially very difficult in terms of the accounting entries. It is much better to have a credit card that you use solely for business expenses, and include this in the business accounts – then all the interest will be allowable, subject to the rule about not overdrawing your capital account described above.

7.25   Partnerships

Instead of being a sole trader, you may set up your property development business as a partnership – trading together with one or more other people, and sharing the risks and rewards with them. If you decide to do this, there are some important tips to bear in mind:

- Have a written partnership agreement – if you do not, then the Partnership Act 1890 will govern how profits and losses are split, and it presumes that they will be split equally between the partners – which may not be what you want.

- Beware of taking children into partnership unless they genuinely contribute to the business – this is something that is currently a "hot topic" with HMRC. Provided the documents are correctly drafted, however, it is very difficult for HMRC to challenge a spouse as partner.

- Take advice from a tax adviser on the finer points of how to deal with the partnership's tax – it can be a complicated area, with traps for the unwary!

- Always take advice before making any changes to the partnership – such as who is a partner, what the profit shares are, and so on – again, beware of pitfalls!

Caution: Always remember that partners are "jointly liable" for the debts of the partnership – if one partner cannot pay, the creditor can go after the others. You need to trust anyone you go into partnership with!

---

8   Taxation for Homeowners

For many people, their home is their most valuable asset, and all the more valuable because they believe that when they sell it, they will make a capital gain that is exempt from tax.

In this part of the guide, we will look at the details of how that tax exemption works, and what pitfalls and opportunities it provides. We will also look at an exemption from income tax on rental income from your home.

We will start with the basic rules, and then look at what can be done with them:

8.1   The Basic Exemption

It is common knowledge that you are exempt from capital gains tax (CGT) on a gain you make from selling your home.

As we shall see, this exemption is a little more complicated than it might appear.

8.2   "Only or Main Residence"

The exemption applies to a person's "only or main residence" (also referred to as one's "Principal Private Residence", or "PPR").

In a simple case where a person owns only one property, lives in it as his home, and does not use it for any other purpose, then when he sells it, he will pay no CGT.

A person can have only one main residence at a time, and a married couple (or civil partnership) can have only one between them.

If a person (or couple) has more than one property that could be regarded as a main residence, they have the opportunity to "nominate" which one the tax relief should apply to. As we shall see, it is <u>vital</u> to make this nomination within the time limit that applies.

From April 2015, you can basically only nominate a property outside the UK as a main residence if you spend at least 90 nights there in the tax year in question. You should seek tailored advice when you intend to claim on a non-UK property, or to claim as a non-resident individual, as the rules and calculations can become complex.

8.3   "Garden or Grounds"

The exemption covers not only the house itself, but also the "permitted area" of the land around it.

Up to half a hectare (about 1.2 acres) of garden is allowed by statute, but a larger area may be included in the exemption if it is "required for the reasonable enjoyment" of the property "having regard to the size and character of the dwelling-house".

The issue of what area of land larger than half a hectare is required for the "reasonable enjoyment" of your home has led to numerous tax cases being tried in the Courts, and it would be pointless to go into the details here as every case is different, but there is one particular point that is worth noticing:

Mr Grey and Mr Green live in similar large houses. Each house has a garden of 1.7 acres.

Mr Grey sells his house (and garden). There is some discussion with the inspector about whether the "extra" half acre (above the 1.2 acre limit) is "required for the reasonable enjoyment" of the property, but the inspector eventually concedes that it is, and the whole gain is exempt.

Mr Green receives an excellent offer to sell a half acre of his garden to a property developer.

He has read about CGT, so he knows that because he still owns the house, the exemption for the garden or grounds can apply to this sale.

He sells the land, and does not expect to pay CGT on the gain he makes.

The tax inspector does not agree, and says that CGT is due on the substantial gain Mr Green made on selling the half acre.

Mr Green objects that when his friend Mr Grey sold a similar house and land, it was accepted that the whole gain was exempt.

"Ah", replies the tax inspector, "but the test must be applied to the exact circumstances of each sale, and to me, the very fact that you are prepared to sell that half acre while you remain living in the house <u>may be prima facie evidence that the part disposed of was not **required** for the reasonable enjoyment of the dwelling house as a residence.</u> So the exemption doesn't apply to it".

(The underlined words above are taken verbatim from HMRC's own CGT Manual at paragraph CG64832).

8.4   Periods of Absence

Generally speaking, a property is only your main residence while you are actually living there, but there are certain exceptions:

- You can be absent for up to three years (either continuously or for several shorter periods up to a total of three years) for any reason, and

- You can be absent for any period during which you are employed in a full-time job outside the UK, and

- You can be absent for up to four years if your place of work makes this necessary (whether you are employed or self-employed)

For any of these three exceptions to apply, there are two conditions which must normally be fulfilled:

- The property must have been your main residence at some time both before and after the period of absence (there are exceptions in some cases)

- You must not have had another main residence during the period of absence (this is one example of how important the "nomination" of your main residence can be).

Case Study - 11   Absences from Main Residence

James Bond buys a house in London in March 1997, and lives in it as his main residence until January 1998. He then leaves the house and is away until he returns to it in December 2000 (he prefers not to say where he was, but during 1998 the inspector of taxes received a letter from him from the Cayman Islands, saying that he had a lease on a flat there and he wished to "nominate" his London property as his main residence).

From January 2001 until December 2006, he is away in Russia, working in the British Embassy in Moscow. He lives in various different hotels – a hotel room cannot normally be a "main residence"

Mr Bond returns to the UK in December 2006, and in January 2007 he sets up a business in the Scottish Highlands, offering "adventure training" and "team building" for business executives. He rents a castle to accommodate this business. He also does another main residence nomination in favour of his London house.

In December 2010, Mr Bond returns to the London house, and moves back in. He lives there until March 2016, when he sells the property.

All of the gain is exempt, because:

- His "unexplained" absence lasted just under three years

- While he was away in Moscow, he had a full-time job there (note there is no time limit for this type of absence)

- He obviously had to live in Scotland while he was running his adventure training centre, and that period lasted just under four years

And the house was his main residence both before and after all of these periods of absence, and he did not have another main residence during any of his absences – or if he did, he had "nominated" the London house.

8.5 "Job-Related Accommodation"

There is a slightly different (and more generous) relief that applies if you live in "job-related accommodation."

This relief is not often available, because the definition of "job-related accommodation" is very strict, so we will not go into detail here.

The object of the relief is to enable someone who <u>has</u> to live in a particular place – such as the manager of a pub required to live on the premises – to buy a house elsewhere (perhaps for his retirement) and have it treated as if it is his main residence even though he has not yet lived there.

In some circumstances, this relief is also available to the self-employed and (in very limited circumstances) to owner/directors of companies.

Provided that it was genuinely your intention to live in the house in the future, it is possible for the house to be sold and the gain to be exempt, even if you have never in fact lived there – but HMRC are likely to look very closely at the facts in such a case.

> **Caution:** A word of caution – if you think you may be in this situation, do not just assume your present accommodation is "job-related" and that you will qualify for this relief – check with a tax adviser, as the rules are strict, complicated, and illogical, like a lot of tax rules.

8.6 "The 18 Month Rule"

If a property has been your main residence <u>at any time</u> while you owned it, it is deemed to be your main residence for the last 18 months of your ownership, whether you live there or not: We shall see how this rule can be made to work for you in a moment.

8.7 Nominating Your Main Residence

If you have more than one property that could be regarded as your main residence, you can "nominate" which property is to get the tax relief by writing to HMRC within two years of the time when the situation first arises.

For example, many people have a family home in one place, and work during the week in another place, where they have a flat. Either of these could be regarded as their residence, so they can nominate which one will get the tax relief.

The two-year time limit is strictly enforced by HMRC, so do not delay in making your nomination. If you miss the deadline, you cannot make a nomination until your situation changes – such as when you acquire another property that could be your main residence.

Note that a rented flat could be regarded as your main residence, so if you rent a flat during the week and return to your home at weekends, you need to nominate the home you own as your main residence. If you are in this situation and have missed the two-year deadline, one solution would be to move to another rented flat – that will start a new two-year period for a nomination. There is also a concessionary treatment that may potentially apply – and may be cheaper than renting another flat.

If you do not nominate which property is your main residence, the issue has to be decided "on the facts of the case". In other words, you may be in for a long and expensive argument with HMRC if they disagree with you about the meaning of those facts!

Once your nomination is in place, you can "vary" it at any time by writing to HMRC again, and the variation can be retrospective for up to two years.

The facility to "nominate" a main residence, and then vary that nomination, can produce some spectacular tax savings:

Case Study - 12   Nominating Your Main Residence

Joe owns a large house in Devon, where he lives with his family. He and his wife bought this house in March 1997. In January 2010, he gets a job in London, and in March 2011, he buys a small studio flat in London for £100,000, where he lives during the working week, returning to Devon most weekends.

Joe writes to HMRC in March 2011, nominating the Devon house as his main residence. His wife has to sign the nomination as well (it affects her too, because a married couple can only have one main residence).

In January 2014, Joe is offered another job, this time in Devon. He gives in his notice at his London job, and while he is working out that notice, he writes to HMRC, saying he wants to vary his nomination, making the London flat his main residence from 1 December 2013.

A week or so later, he writes again, saying he wishes to vary the nomination yet again, to make the Devon house his main residence from 1 January 2014. His wife signs both these nominations as well, remember. Joe sells the London flat for £160,000 in March 2014, making a gain of £60,000. Because of the way he has varied his nomination, the flat was his main residence for tax purposes for one month (December 2013).

This means that the last 18 months of his ownership of it are exempt from CGT under the "last 18 months" rule. As he has only owned the flat for three years, half the gain is exempt from CGT.

When Joe and his wife eventually come to sell the Devon house, it will have been their main residence for the whole period of ownership, except for that one month in December 2013, so only a small fraction of the gain will not be exempt from CGT.

If, say, they sell it in March 2017, they will have owned it for 20 years, which is 240 months, so only 1/240th of the gain will not be exempt – even if they made a gain of £500,000, only £2,083 of that would be taxable, and their annual exempt amounts will cover that (each of Joe and his wife are entitled to £11,100 tax free capital gains in 2016/17.

8.8   Relief for Letting

If a property has been your main residence, and at some other stage in your ownership it has been let as "residential accommodation", then there is a further relief from CGT on the part of the gain that is attributable to the period of letting.

The relief is the <u>smallest</u> of:

- The gain due to the letting
- The amount of the gain that is exempt as your main residence
- £40,000

The relief also applies where you own a house and let part of it throughout the time you own it.

Case Study - 13   Relief for Letting

Chris buys a house in January 2007, and lives in it as his main residence until December 2008.

He then lets it from January 2009 until December 2015, when he sells the house, making a gain of £160,000.

He has owned the house for 8 years.

For 3 1/2 years, it has been his main residence (2007 and 2008, when he actually lived there, and July 2014 to December 2015, under the "last 18 months" rule).

7/16 of the gain (£70,000) is therefore exempt, leaving a chargeable gain of £90,000.

The amount of the lettings exemption is therefore the smallest of:

- The gain due to the letting = £90,000

- The amount of the exemption for main residence given = £70,000

- The maximum amount of the exemption = £40,000

Chris gets the maximum exemption of £40,000, leaving only £50,000 taxable.

If Chris were married and his wife owned the house jointly with him, the gain would be split between them, and each of them would be entitled to their own letting relief of up to £40,000:

	Chris	Wife	Total
Gain	80,000	80,000	160,000
7/16 exempt as main residence	(35,000)	(35,000)	(70,000)

Taxable	45,000	45,000	90,000
Lettings relief = lowest of Taxable = 45,000 OMR exemption = 35,000 Maximum relief = 40,000	(35,000)	(35,000)	(70,000)
Chargeable gain (covered by £11,100 annual exemption)	10,000	10,000	20,000

An important point to notice is that this relief can also apply where *part* of the house is let throughout most (but not all) of the period of ownership:

Case Study - 14   Lettings Relief for B&B

John buys a large house, with five bedrooms.

After a year during which he used the whole house as his main residence and used the extra bedrooms when he gave parties, he lets three of these out as Bed and Breakfast accommodation, and lives in the rest of the house as his main residence. He sells the house and makes a gain of £250,000.

It is agreed with HMRC that the B&B bedrooms represent 30% of the value of the house, so 70% of the gain (£175,000) is exempt and 30% (£75,000) is taxable.

The letting relief is the smallest of:

- Taxable due to letting = £75,000

- Exempt as main residence = £175,000

- Maximum relief = £40,000

So £40,000 relief is given, leaving John with a taxable gain of £35,000.

NOTE: When it is applied to businesses such as Hotels, Guest Houses, and B&Bs, this relief depends on the let rooms being part of the same "dwelling house" as the main residence.

In John's case this was simple – it was one big house and he let three rooms in it.

There can be problems where the owner effectively lives in a self-contained flat within the building, as then HMRC may argue that his "dwelling house" is the flat, not the whole building.

This is a complicated area, and you should seek advice from a Tax Adviser if there is any doubt as to what constitutes your "dwelling house".

8.9 Income Tax Relief for Letting

Normally, if you let part of your house, you will be liable to income tax on the rental income (less expenses – more on this later), but there is a relief called "Rent a Room" relief which can apply to exempt up to **£7,500** of rent, per year, from tax. (It was increased in the Summer 2015 Budget, from £4,250, with effect from 6 April 2016)

The relief applies if your tenant lives with you (as with a lodger), or if they have a self-contained part of the house, <u>provided the separation of their part is only temporary, and does not involve structural alterations.</u>

The relief is not compulsory – you can elect not to have it if you wish:

Case Study - 15   Rent a Room Relief

Anne, Barry, and Chris are next door neighbours, each living in a terraced house. During the tax year 2016/17 (the year ending 5 April 2017), they each have a lodger.

Anne's lodger pays her £120 per week. Her expenses (including an appropriate proportion of the mortgage interest on the house) are £1,200

Barry's lodger pays £175 per week, to include meals. Barry has no mortgage, and his expenses are £1,000

Chris' lodger pays him the same as Barry's, but because he has a very large mortgage, and provides more expensive food, etc., for the lodger, his expenses are £8,400 for the year.

Anne's profit from the rental is £5,040 (£6,240 less £1,200). She is exempt from tax on this, as the rental income (not the profit) was less than the Rent a Room limit of £7,500.

There is no point in her electing for the relief not to apply, as then she would be taxed on £5,040. Only in the unlikely event that you make a loss is it worth opting out of the scheme if your rents are less than the limit.

Barry's rental income is above the £7,500 limit. He has a choice:

- He can pay tax on his actual profit of £8,100 (£9,100 less £1,000 actual expenses) or

- He can elect to be taxed on the excess of his gross rental income received over the Rent a Room limit - £9,100 less £7,500 = £1,600. Clearly, this is the best choice for him

Like Barry, Chris' income is above the limit, so he has the same choice:

- Tax on actual profit of £700 (52 x £175 = £9,100 less £8,400 = £700

- Tax on rents less £7,500 = £9,100 - £7,500 = £1,600

Chris will not elect for the relief to apply, as he is better off paying tax as if it did not exist.

NOTE 1: Whether or not you need to make an election depends on whether your rental income (not your profit) is above or below the limit for the year of £7,500.

- If it is below £7,500, you will be in the scheme unless you elect for it not to apply to you (perhaps because you have made a loss)

- If it is above £7,500, you will not be in the scheme and will be taxed in the normal way (income less allowable expenses) unless you elect to be in (probably because your actual expenses were less than £7,500, like Barry's)

NOTE 2: The £7,500 limit applies to one person's income from letting part of his main residence.

If the residence is shared and another person also gets rental income from the same residence, the amount of relief for each individual is reduced to £3,750 – so if Anne, Barry, and Chris shared one big house, and they had a lodger, their rent a room relief would be £3,750 each.

8.10   Restrictions on Main Residence Relief

We have already seen that relief from CGT for your main residence can be restricted if you let part of it, or if there is a period when it is not your main residence.

A similar restriction applies where you use part of the property <u>exclusively</u> for the purposes of a business – a good example is a pub where the owner lives on the premises.

The apportionment is to be done on a "just and reasonable" basis:

Case Study - 16   Apportionment

The "Tax Inspector's Head" is a popular pub, owned and run by Mr Porter.

It consists of a ground floor with two bars, a ladies' and a gents' lavatory, a storeroom-cum-beer cellar and a kitchen that is used both to prepare pub food and to cook meals for the Porter family. There are six rooms upstairs, used as their main residence by the Porter family, except for one small room which is Mr Porter's office.

When working out how to apportion the gain when the pub is sold, the following points will be relevant:

- The floor areas of the various rooms

- The fact that it is probably true that a significant part of the sale price was for the goodwill of the pub business (so not eligible for main residence relief)

- The kitchen should be treated as part of the main residence, not the business (because it was not used "exclusively" for the business as the Porters' own meals were cooked there)

- Mr Porter may argue that his office was not "exclusively" used as such and should also be excluded from the business – this will depend on the facts of the case.

8.11 Withdrawal of Main Residence Relief

There is a dangerous piece of legislation (Section 224 (3) of the Taxation of Chargeable Gains Act 1992), which says that the relief from CGT for a main residence:

"...shall not apply in relation to a gain if the acquisition of, or of the interest in, the dwelling house or the part of a dwelling house was made wholly or partly for the purpose of realising a gain from the disposal of it, and shall not apply in relation to a gain so far as attributable to any expenditure which was incurred after the beginning of the period of ownership and was incurred wholly or partly for the purpose of realising a gain from the disposal"

Just take a moment and read that through again, and then we shall have a look at what it means in practice.

Essentially it seems to say that you don't get the CGT exemption at all if one of your reasons ("wholly or partly") for buying the house was that you hoped you would make a profit when you eventually sold it, and also that if you spend money on improvements (new conservatory, swimming pool, etc.) and one of your reasons for that is to increase the value of the house, then you lose the exemption on that increase in value.

Fortunately, HMRC do not apply this legislation as strictly as that – their own instruction manual tells inspectors not to be "unreasonable and restrictive" in the way they apply this rule.

Merely because you buy a house hoping it will increase in value, or because you improve it partly because this will improve the selling price, you will not fall foul of this rule.

Examples where you will are:

- Pseudo property dealing

- "Enfranchisement" of a leasehold property shortly before sale

- Property development involving your home

We will look at these in turn:

8.12 Pseudo Property Dealing

If you buy a property intending to sell it in the short term at a profit, this is normally a trading activity, but if you buy the property and live in it as your main residence, it is very difficult for HMRC to argue that you bought it as trading stock.

For example, a builder might buy a property to live in, spend a few months improving it, sell it on for a gain and claim that it was his only or main residence and that the gain should not be taxed.

HMRC may struggle to say that he is trading, because it may genuinely be his main residence for a few months or so, but they will then use section 224 (3) to deny him the main residence exemption for the capital gains he makes on each house.

We shall shortly be looking at exactly what makes a property your main residence, and the thorny question of how long you have to live there to get the relief, but at this point, notice that even if you do live at the house so that it is your main residence, if you only own the property for a short time, you may be vulnerable to losing the exemption on the basis that you bought the property with a view to making a gain on selling it.

8.13 Enfranchisement of Leasehold Property

If you are a leasehold tenant, you may get the opportunity to buy the freehold from your landlord and thus "enfranchise" your property. Especially if your lease does not have many years to run, this can considerably increase the value of your property.

If you then sell the property within the next couple of years or so, HMRC may well argue that the cost of buying the freehold was "incurred wholly or partly for the purpose of realising a gain from the disposal".

You will of course argue that you had no thought of selling at the time, and you just wanted security, and the opportunity to leave the house to your children, but the shorter the period between enfranchisement and sale, the harder this argument will be to justify.

If it is agreed that you did ("partly") think in terms of a bigger profit when you sold, the restriction on your relief will be calculated like this:

Case Study - 17   Enfranchisement

Fred lives in a leasehold property which is his main residence. The lease, which now has 65 years left to run, cost him £70,000 ten years ago. He gets the opportunity to buy the freehold for £80,000, does so, and sells the house freehold for £200,000.

After negotiations with HMRC, it is agreed that if he had not enfranchised his property, and had merely sold the 65 year lease, he would only have got £75,000 for the property.

The calculation is therefore:

Sale proceeds of freehold	200,000
Sale proceeds if leasehold only	(75,000)
Gain attributable to enfranchisement	125,000
Cost of buying freehold	(80,000)
Gain not exempt from CGT	45,000

The rest of the gain is exempt as his main residence.

NOTE: This Case Study provides the opportunity to make an important point about tax planning.

Fred will pay CGT on this £45,000 gain of about £9,500, so he has over £110,000 in the bank, after taking account of the cost of the freehold and the CGT. If he had simply sold his lease, he would have had £75,000.

JUST BECAUSE YOU WILL PAY MORE TAX IF YOU UNDERTAKE A TRANSACTION, THAT DOESN'T MEAN YOU SHOULD NOT DO IT – If you will still be better off after the extra tax, then tax is no reason not to go ahead!

9 Property Development of Your Home

This is the third scenario where the restriction on relief may apply. The commonest example is where the owner of a large home divides it up into flats before selling:

Case Study - 18   Home Divided into Flats

Barney owns a large three storey house, which he lives in as his main residence. It cost him £100,000 twenty years ago.

He decides to sell, and his estate agent suggests that if he splits the property up into three self-contained flats, he will realise a better price than he would get if he sold the house as it is.

Barney spends £50,000 on dividing the house into three flats, and then sells them for £150,000 each. If he had just sold the house as it was, he would have got £300,000 for it.

The non-exempt part of the gain is calculated like this:

Sale proceeds of three flats	450,000
Sale proceeds if house sold unconverted	(300,000)
Gain attributable to conversion	150,000
Less cost of conversion	(50,000)
Gain not exempt	100,000

The gain that Barney would have made if he had just sold his property unconverted remains tax-free. Barney might also want to read point 7.8 above, to secure reduced rates of VAT for construction costs when changing the number of dwellings.

9.1   Selling the Garden

Sometimes it is possible to sell part of your garden, perhaps to a property developer. If the total area of your garden before this sale is less than half a hectare (about 1.2 acres) then, assuming the house is your main residence, a gain on the sale of part of the garden will be exempt from CGT.

This only works if the house is your main residence <u>at the time you sell the piece of garden.</u>

Mary's main residence has a garden of one acre. She is planning to sell the house, and she receives an offer from a developer to buy a half acre of the garden.

While she is still negotiating with the developer, she receives an offer for the house and the remaining half acre of garden, which she accepts.

Mary exchanges contracts to sell the house on 1 March 2014, and the house is conveyed to its new owner on 21 March 2014. This gain will be exempt from CGT, because the house was Mary's main residence.

She finally agrees terms with the developer on 1 April 2014, and sells him the half acre. The capital gain on this sale is NOT exempt from CGT, because <u>at the time of the sale,</u> the land was not part of the garden of her main residence (because she had already sold the house).

If only Mary had sold the garden to the developer first, and then sold the house, both gains would have been exempt from CGT.

NOTE: The date of a sale for CGT purposes is the date contracts are exchanged rather than the date the sale is completed. If, however, Mary had sold the garden on 10 March (after she had exchanged contracts to sell the house, but before she moved out of it when completion of the sale took place on 21 March) HMRC would have accepted that the garden was still part of her main residence on 10 March and the gain would have been exempt.

9.2   What is a "Main Residence"?

Throughout this section we have been talking about a person's "main residence", but what exactly does this term mean?

Your main residence may be a house, or a flat.

You may own the freehold, have a lease, or merely be renting it, perhaps as a Shorthold Tenant.

<u>Note:</u> even rented property can be a main residence for tax purposes, and so (subject to certain restrictions – see 8.2 above) can a property outside the UK.

In order to be your main residence, a property must be occupied by you as your home, but it need not be occupied every day – see also 8.4.

A question often asked is how long it is necessary to live in a property before it becomes your main residence, but unfortunately it is impossible to answer that question, although in the right circumstances the period of occupation can be as little as a few months, or even less.

What is important is not so much the length of time, but more the quality of your occupation of the property.

Case Study - 20   A Main Residence for a week

Jack exchanges contracts to buy a small flat on 1 August, and the sale completes and he moves in on 21 August. He fully intends to make the flat his home, but on 28 August he wins £1,000,000 on the lottery.

Jack lets the flat while he goes on a world cruise for three months, and on his return he buys a large house to live in, and sells the flat.

HMRC might be a little suspicious, but provided they could be convinced that Jack really intended to live in the flat when he bought it, and that he did actually live there for the week before he won the lottery, then any gain Jack makes on the sale of the flat should be exempt from CGT. The key point is that, when Jack rolled up on 21 August, he occupied the property as his home and his demonstrable intention at the time was to live there, for the foreseeable future.

People who own a rental property they have never lived in are often advised to move into it before selling it, in order to get the "last 18 months" exemption and the £40,000 "lettings exemption":

Case Study - 21   The Last 18 Months Exemption

Mark and Mandy own a house which they have never lived in, but have let out. They also own their main residence. The let house cost £100,000 in May 2008. In May 2016, Mark and Mandy let out their main residence, and move into the house they had previously been letting. They live there for a year, and then sell the house in May 2017 for £400,000. The gain is calculated like this:

Sale proceeds	400,000
Less cost	(100,000)
Gain	300,000
Main residence exemption (last 18 months) 1&1/2 out of 9 years (i.e. 1/6) exempt	(50,000)
Lettings exemption (max'd at main exemption)	(50,000)
Chargeable gain	200,000
Annual exempt amounts	(22,200)

Gain charged to tax	177,800
CGT at 28%	49,784

If Mark and Mandy had not lived in the house before they sold it, their gain would have been £300,000. After their annual exempt amounts were deducted, they would pay CGT of £77,784.

By moving in for a year, they have saved themselves £28,000 in tax!

Mark and Mandy let out their old main residence, and genuinely lived in the previously let house for a year, so they are entitled to the exemptions shown above.

It is essential that you actually live in a property if you are going to claim it is your main residence. If you have another property that could be regarded as your main residence as well, **do not forget to "nominate" which one is to be your main residence** for tax purposes.

Case Study - 22   Not a Real Main Residence?

Sam and Sally are in a similar situation to Mark and Mandy – they have a main residence, and they also have a let property.

They intend to sell the let property, and they have been told that if they make it their main residence before sale, they will enjoy the same tax savings that Mark and Mandy did.

Unfortunately, the let house is some 50 miles from their main residence, in a rather run-down neighbourhood, and inconvenient for commuting to work.

They get rid of the tenant, and spend a few weekends in the ex-rental property, having nominated it as their main residence (they are "in time" to make the nomination on the basis that the let property only became a possible main residence after the tenant left and it became available for them to occupy).

They do not bother to move any of their furniture or other possessions into the house, making do with the (rather dilapidated) furniture provided for the tenant when the house was let.

They do not let their main residence, because they need it during the week, and they do not notify their bank, their employers, or anyone else of their change of address. After six months of this, they sell the ex-rental property, and claim the same reliefs as Mark and Mandy.

The inspector of taxes raises an enquiry into their tax returns, and when the above facts come out, he announces that, in his opinion, their move to the ex-rental property was a sham, and it was never their main residence, so none of the reliefs enjoyed by Mark and Mandy are due.

Depending on how half-hearted their occupation of the ex-rental property was, the inspector might even argue that their tax returns were incorrect because of "deliberate and concealed inaccuracy", and seek penalties based on a percentage of the tax they tried to avoid paying (or, in this case, it could be argued, "evade" paying!).

This may seem an extreme example, but we frequently deal with clients who have previously been advised that "all you need to do is make sure the utility bills are in your name and say you were living there" ... this falls well short of the quality of occupation required.

10 Buy to Let ("BTL")

This sector has grown hugely in the last ten years or so. In this chapter we will look at the various ways that rental income can be generated from property, and the way that the profits from the letting will be taxed. We will also look at the tax implications of selling your buy to let property.

10.1 Income from property

If you own and let property, you will be liable to income tax on the profit you make, after taking account of the expenses you have to pay.

Income tax is charged at the following rates for 2016/17, according to your total income for the tax year:

First £11,000	Nil (this is your "personal allowance")
Next £32,000	20% (the "basic rate")
£32,001 to £150,000	40% (the "higher rate")
Over £150,000	45% (the "additional rate")

Note that, for taxable incomes over £100,000, the personal allowance is progressively withdrawn, producing a marginal rate of tax of 60% on income between £100,000 and £122,000.

10.2 Capital v Revenue, and "Wholly and Exclusively"

These distinctions are just as relevant for a buy to let landlord as they are for a property developer – see paragraphs 7.12 and 7.13.

10.3 Allowable Expenses

If you have a buy to let property, you can deduct the following expenses from the rent you receive in order to calculate your taxable profits (always assuming they pass the "wholly and exclusively" test referred to above):

- Advertising for tenants for your property – but not the cost of advertising your property for sale, as this would be a capital expense (potentially deductible for CGT purposes)

- Bad debts

- Cost of providing services to tenants – for example, if you do the gardening, or keep the common parts of the property clean, the cost of this can be deducted

- Interest on loans for the purposes of the business, and the cost of obtaining them – but with an important caveat that the rules for claiming interest relief on buy-to-let residential lettings are about to change from April 2017, with serious consequences for any residential landlord who has significant borrowings or finance costs.

- Rent collection

- Staff costs

- Repairs to the let property

- Rent paid – if you are not the owner of the property, and you rent it then sublet it

- Rates (on commercial property), Water bills, and Council Tax – but only if you pay these rather than your tenant paying them

- Insurance of the property, its contents, and for loss of rents

- Legal and professional fees

- Travelling expenses

We need to look at some of the above expenses in more detail:

10.4   Bad Debts

Strictly speaking, the accounts for your BTL business should be prepared on the "accruals" basis (also sometimes known as the "earnings basis"). Using this method, you account for income as it "accrues" and expenditure as you "incur" it:

Case Study - 23   Accruals Basis

Dawn has a portfolio of two rental properties. She prepares the accounts for her business to 5 April each year.

The rent on her two properties is payable six monthly in advance, and during the year she puts the rent up as shown below. The tenant of property B disputes the increase, and withholds payment of the rent due on 1 July 2016 and 1 January 2017 in protest.

Months	Property A	Property B
Jan 16 to June 16 Due 1 Jan 16	600 per month	700 per month
July 16 to Dec 16 Due 1 July 16	700 per month	800 per month (unpaid at 5 April 2017)

Jan 17 to June 17 Due 1 January 17	700 per month	800 per month (unpaid at 5 April 2017)

To find the rent for property A for the year ending 5 April 2017, we need to look at the rent over the period:

The rent for the period 1 January 2016 to 30 June 2016 was 600 x 6 = 3,600, so for the period 6 April to 30 June it was 3,600 divided by 181 times 86 = 1,710.

For the period 1 July 2016 to 30 June 2017, the rent was 700 x 12 = 8,400, so for the period 1 July 2016 to 5 April 2017 it was 8,400 divided by 365 times 279 = 6,421.

The total rent for Property A for the tax year to 5 April 2017 is thus 1,710 plus 6,421 = 8,131.

We use the same method for property B, so we get:

6 April 2016 to 30 June 2016 = 1,996
1 July 2016 to 5 April 2017 = 7,338
Total rent for year to 5 April 2017 = 9,334

Total of rent from both properties = 17,465

17,465 is the figure to be included for rental income in Dawn's accounts, despite the fact that the rent on property B has not been paid for the period from 1 January 2017 to 5 April 2017.

Dawn now needs to consider if the tenant of property B will *ever* pay the rent he owes.

If she has good reason to believe he will never pay her, she can claim an expense for the unpaid amount as a Bad Debt – but only if there were good grounds on 5 April 2017 for believing that the rent would not be paid, and if it has in fact not been paid by the time she prepares her accounts.

If a deduction is claimed for such a bad debt, and it is then recovered at a later date, the amount recovered must be treated as income received at the time the debt is paid.

The same applies to expenses:

The insurance for the two properties is paid annually in advance, on 1 August. For the period in question, the premiums were:

1 August 2015 (for year to 31 July 2016) = 1,100
1 August 2016 (for year to 31 July 2017) = 950

For the year ending 5 April 2017, therefore, the amount to be included in the accounts for insurance is:

Period 5 April 2016 to 31 July 2016 = 1,100 divided by 365 times 117 = 353
Period 1 August 2016 to 5 April 2017 = 950 divided by 365 times 248 = 645
Total for year to 5 April 2017 = 998

NOTE: The apportionment of expenses above has been done on a daily basis to highlight how the principle works; in practice, the 5 days in April can be ignored and the apportionment can be done on a monthly basis (i.e. for the year ending 31 March 2017 in this case), provided this is done consistently from year to year, and provided that it does not make a significant difference to the result.

10.5   Cash Basis

The 2013 Finance Act included provision for traders (and landlords) with turnover below the VAT registration limit (£83,000 for 2016/17) to prepare their accounts on the basis of cash received and cash spent, but this is unlikely to be of interest to landlords, because if you choose to use the "cash basis" you are not allowed to deduct more than £500 of interest paid on loans.

10.6   Loft and Cavity Wall Insulation

Assuming there was no such insulation beforehand, the cost of this would be a capital expense (because it would be an improvement to the property), but there **was** a specific relief (the "Landlord's Energy Saving Allowance") which allowed up to £1,500 to be claimed towards the cost of installing this in an existing building that was let, or going to be let, within six months.

This relief has been abolished for expenditure after 5 April 2015. New installations will no longer be allowed, but if you have incurred such expenses before the Allowance was abolished, you may now be able to claim "Overpayment Relief". The cost of replacing insulation will generally remain allowable as a repair.

10.7   Rent Collection

If you pay an agency to deal with the letting of your property, their fees are allowable, as are any similar costs associated with the collection of rent, such as the cost of suing a tenant for rent arrears.

10.8   Staff Costs

If you employ anyone to help you in your rental business, the cost of their pay is an allowable deduction, subject to the "wholly and exclusively" principle. If, for example, you employ a gardener/handyman who does work on your own home as well as on your buy to lets, you should apportion his pay on a reasonable basis between his work on the BTL properties (allowable), and on your home (not allowable). Likewise employing a family member would be an allowable expense, provided the payment was commensurate with the work undertaken.

Note that you cannot claim a deduction for the time you, the landlord, spend working for the business.

If your property is owned through a limited company, however, the position is different – see my guide **"Tax Dos and Don'ts for Property Companies"**, available through the Property Tax Portal.

10.9 Repairs and Renewals

This can be a minefield! The basic principle has already been stated:

Repairs are revenue expenses, and allowable against rents, but improvements are capital expenditure, and not allowable against rents.

The problems arise when we are at the borderline between a repair and an improvement:

Case Study - 24   Repairs, Improvements, and "The Entirety"

Bill and Ben are both BTL landlords. Bill owns a two bedroom house he lets out, and so does Ben. In order not to complicate this case study, they have both kindly agreed not to insure their properties against storm damage!

One day, a severe storm destroys the roofs of both properties.

Bill pays to have the roof replaced with a similar one – this costs him £8,000.

Ben takes the opportunity to have the loft of the house converted into a new flat, raising the height of the walls by one metre. The cost of this is £30,000.

Bill is allowed a deduction for the whole of the £8,000. He has replaced the damaged roof with a similar one, and this is a repair.

Ben gets no deduction at all for his £30,000. This is because the conversion of the loft is clearly an improvement, and the replacement roof is part of the "entirety" of that improvement.

This may seem unfair, but the facts in Ben's case are based on one of the leading cases on the subject of repairs *(Thomas Wilson (Keighly) Ltd v Emerson, in 1960).*

10.10 "Notional Repairs"

There used to be a concession, whereby in a case like Ben's a claim would have been accepted for "notional repairs" – that is, for the cost of repairs that were no longer necessary because of the improvements. Under this concession, Ben could have been given a deduction for the £8,000 he would otherwise have had to spend on repairing the roof.

Caution: This concession was withdrawn from April 2001, and "notional repairs" can no longer be claimed in such cases.

10.11 Modern Materials

Sometimes it is almost impossible, or impractical, to repair a property by replacing "like with like" as Bill did. Perhaps the best example is double glazing.

If your BTL property has old fashioned single-glazed windows, and these need replacing, it is likely to be necessary to install modern double glazing rather than to have replacement single-glazed windows made. In a case like this, where the "improvement" is a result of modern materials and techniques, HMRC will usually accept that the expenditure is on a repair (allowable), not an improvement.

10.12 Repairing Newly-Acquired Property

If you buy a BTL property that is in a dilapidated state, then it is possible that the cost of putting it right may be regarded as capital expenditure (in effect, part of the cost of buying the property itself) and so not be allowed as an expense against the rent.

This is likely to be the case if:

- The property was not in a fit state to be let when you bought it, so the improvements were necessary to make it possible to use it in your business, or

- The price of the property was significantly reduced as a result of its poor condition

In other cases, however, repairs before the first letting are an allowable expense – note that there is a common misconception that they are not allowable.

10.13 Legal and Professional Fees

Whether these are allowable depends on whether they are associated with capital or revenue expenditure.

The following legal and professional fees are capital, and so cannot be deducted from the rent (although some may be deductible for CGT purposes):

- Fees relating to the purchase of the property

- Fees relating to the first letting of a property, if the lease is for more than one year

- Fees for getting planning permission

- Fees relating to the sale of the property

The following are of a revenue nature, and so can be deducted from the rent:

- Fees relating to the first letting of the property where the lease is for less than a year

- Fees connected with the renewal of a lease (provided it is for less than 50 years)

- Insurance valuations

- Accountancy costs for preparing rental accounts and tax computations

- Subscriptions to associations representing the interests of landlords

- The costs associated with rent reviews or arbitration

- The costs of evicting a bad tenant (if he is to be replaced with a new one, but not if the property is to be sold)

10.14 Furniture, etc.

In general, a landlord of furnished residential property cannot claim a deduction for **capital expenditure** on such things as:

- Cookers

- Electrical appliances

- Furniture

- Carpets and curtains

- Cutlery and crockery

As an alternative, he could claim a "wear and tear" allowance (but see below):

10.15 Renewals Allowance aka Replacement Furniture Relief

It used to be possible to claim the cost of replacing the sort of items listed above, albeit not the cost of buying the original ones, but HMRC decided – with very little warning – to stop allowing this treatment for expenditure incurred after 5 April 2013.

There has been considerable dispute from the tax profession about whether HMRC had the statutory power to refuse to accept the renewals basis, and in the end the government decided to introduce something called "Replacement Furniture Relief", that looks, sounds and smells very much like the Renewals Basis they said they'd abolished. The "new" relief applies from April 2016.

> **Caution:** NEVER TRY TO APPLY COMMON SENSE TO TAX. Tax, like the past, is a foreign country; they do things differently there!

10.16 Wear and Tear Allowance

Up until April 2016, a landlord of a furnished residential property could deduct 10% of the "net rent" each year. The "net rent" means the rent receivable, less any expenses which are normally borne by a tenant, but are borne by the landlord (such as council tax, water/sewerage charges, and so on). The Allowance was basically intended to meet the landlord's extra costs in providing furniture, and 10% was felt to be a reasonable approximation.

Gordon buys a BTL property and furnishes it. He lets it for £900 per month, and agrees that he will pay the council tax and the water rates on the property. These come to £1,400 per year.

The wear and tear allowance he can claim is £940 per year:

Gross Rents	10,800
Less tenant's costs paid by landlord	(1,400)
Net Rent	9,400
10% of Net Rent	940

Unfortunately, Wear and Tear Allowance has been abolished with effect from April 2016. It is now possible only to claim the actual costs of replacing furniture (or repairing it), using Replacement Furniture Relief.

10.17 Renewals and Wear & Tear Allowance - Scope

You must remember that the Wear and Tear allowance was designed only to cover the sort of items provided by the landlord of a furnished letting that would normally be provided by the tenant of an unfurnished property – see the list of examples above. It did not cover items that are effectively part of the property, such as central heating systems, baths, washbasins, water tanks, and so on. The cost of replacing these can be claimed as a repair, provided it does not comprise a capital improvement. Replacing fixtures such as these is considered a repair to the fabric of the building itself, just like mending a broken window.

10.18 Capital Allowances (CAs)

For information about capital allowances and cars, please see 7.16.

CAs can also be claimed on other machinery and plant used for a rental business. They cannot be claimed on machinery or plant which forms part of a building let as residential property, but they can be claimed on such items as:

- Cars (see 7.16)

- Office equipment and machinery

- Computers

- Tools used for maintenance

- Plant in the common parts of residential property such as apartment blocks, for example lifts and central heating in the lobby, stairwell, etc.

See section 7.18 for more details of Capital Allowances.

In the case of **commercial** property, (and Furnished Holiday Lets) it is often possible to claim substantial capital allowances on certain types of plant and machinery installed in the building.

10.19 Flat Conversion Allowances

Flat Conversion Allowance has been abolished for expenditure incurred after April 2013. A good example of "use it or lose it": very few people claimed it, so it was abolished.

10.20 Losses

Basically, all of the lettings you have are regarded as one business for the purposes of tax, so if you make a loss on one letting (perhaps because of a large mortgage), that loss can be set against your rental income from your other properties.

If you have no other properties, or if there is still some loss left after setting it off against the income from them, then the remaining loss can be carried forward to the next tax year, and the next, and so on, for as long as you are a landlord, until it has been relieved against letting income.

Losses on lettings cannot normally be set against any other income of the year (such as your salary, profits from your trade or profession, or other investment income such as bank interest).

The only exception to this is where part of the loss includes capital allowances – these capital allowances can be set off against your other income for the year of the loss and the following year.

10.21 "Partnerships" and Letting Property

It is not unusual for there to be more than one owner of a let property. Sometimes this is described by those concerned as a "partnership", but you should be aware that HMRC take the view that in the case of a typical investment property with more than one owner, the business is a "joint venture" rather than a partnership.

Their logic for this is that what they call the "passive" letting of property is not sufficiently "business-like" for the property owners to be "persons carrying on a business in common with a view to profit" – this is the definition of a partnership in Section 1 of the Partnership Act 1890.

Given that HMRC recognise that joint owners of property may agree to divide the letting profit between them in any way they choose (and not necessarily in the same proportions as their ownership of the property), this may not seem important, but in the case of a married couple or a civil partnership, there can be a problem.

Where a property is jointly owned by a married couple or a civil partnership, the legislation requires that they be taxed on the rental profit in one of two ways:

- 50% each, regardless of their actual shares of the ownership of the property, OR

- According to their actual ownership of the property, if this is not 50:50 and they elect for this treatment by submitting a "Form 17" to HMRC

Whereas other joint owners can agree to divide the rental profits in any proportion they wish, a married couple (or civil partnership) must use one of the above two methods to apportion the income between them.

10.22 Travelling Expenses

See section 7.15 for details.

10.23 Finance Costs for Residential Property Investors

At the time of writing (2016/17) finance costs are fully deductible so long as they relate to the letting business – are incurred "wholly and exclusively" for the property business (or are apportioned if appropriate). But from April 2017 (the 2017/18 tax year) interest relief will start to be disallowed for tax purposes only. This is nothing to do with private use, but an industry-wide crackdown on easy finance and tax relief.

The government's reasoning for introducing the measure – that it was to eliminate landlords' unfair advantage against budding private homeowners – holds about as much water as my dad's string vest: I don't see the government rushing out to slap tax restrictions on cab drivers, hairdressers, train operators or any other of the countless businesses that 'compete' with me for private activities but expect tax relief for financing their capital expenditure. But it seems that the measures will be implemented, nonetheless.

The key points are:
- The regime applies to all taxpayers that pay income tax – individuals, partners, trusts but **not** companies (which pay 20% corporation tax anyway)
- It tries to catch any kind of financing deal, not just a simple 'mortgage'
- It tries to catch any kind of financial cost, not just 'interest'
- It applies to residential properties and commercial properties are ignored
- Where there are borrowings against both commercial and residential properties, the amount to be disallowed should be apportioned in a "just and reasonable way"
- While property developers are not generally caught, someone financing the development of a property with the intention of letting it out, rather than for onward sale, is subject to the new rules
- Each tax year from 2017/18 through to 2020/21, a further 25% of the landlord's finance costs will be disallowed, to be replaced by a 20% tax credit, regardless of the landlord's actual marginal tax rate

James has 4 residential BTL properties, on which he makes a total of £12,000 profits a year, net of all costs including interest. His interest-only mortgage costs him £1,000 a month. He has a job, earning £30,000 a year. His results are as follows:

Tax Year:	2016/17 £	2017/18 £	2018/19 £	2019/20 £	2020/21 £
Earnings	30,000	30,000	30,000	30,000	30,000
Net Rent after Mortgage	12,000	12,000	12,000	12,000	12,000
Add-back Rental Finance	0	3,000	6,000	9,000	12,000
Total	42,000	45,000	48,000	51,000	54,000
Tax Liability					
Original	6,200	6,800	8,000	9,200	10,400
Rental 20% Tax Credit	0	-600	-1,200	-1,800	-2,400
Net Tax	6,200	6,200	6,800	7,400	8,000
Tax increase on 2016/17	0	0	600	1,200	1,800

There is no disallowance in 2016/17 and, in 2017/18, when 25% of his mortgage interest is disallowed, it actually takes him to the Higher Rate threshold but no further, so he pays extra tax at only 20% and the new tax credit is sufficient to wipe out the extra tax on his rental income. When half of his interest costs are disallowed in 2017/18, however, the extra £3,000 brought into charge takes him over the 40% threshold, so the extra 20% tax credit offsets only half of the additional tax – and so on through to 2020/21, where he is paying an extra £1,800 in tax – basically a tax rate of 60% on his rental income.

While property developers are not directly caught by the regime, they should be very careful if they develop property and then decide to let it out, either because they prefer the property as a long-term investment, or because they are struggling to sell it.

If you think you may be caught by these new rules, then we strongly recommend that you speak to a tax adviser to discuss your options: it is not an exaggeration to say that there are several businesses, otherwise perfectly viable, that will not survive these new measures, simply because the mortgage costs are too high. Please see Chapter 8 (offsetting interest charges before 6th April 2017 and Chapter 9 (offsetting interest charges after 6th April 2017) of the book called "How to Avoid Landlord Taxes".

10.24 Financing the Property & Developments

The costs of taking out a loan to buy a rental property (such as bank fees, commissions, guarantee fees, and valuation fees for security purposes) are an allowable expense – subject to the new rules above.

The same applies to interest paid on such a loan, and to interest paid on other loans, overdrafts and HP agreements, provided the loan was used to buy an asset used in the business.

Where an asset is only used partly for the business, then it may be possible to claim a proportion of the interest on a loan used to buy it.

You cannot claim loan interest if you are taking advantage of the "Rent a Room" allowance of £7,500 (or £3,750 if there is more than one person receiving rent for the property).

The allowability of loan interest can provide a tax efficient way of raising cash for private expenditure:

Case Study - 27   Equity Release/Refinancing

Gordon Brown owns a house that is his main residence.

He bought it in 1998 for £100,000, and there is currently a mortgage outstanding on the property of £45,000.

He is offered a new job in Outer Mongolia, and decides he will let his house while he is away.

The house is now worth £300,000. Gordon renegotiates the mortgage on the house to convert it to a buy to let mortgage, and borrows a further £150,000, which he uses entirely for private expenses – say, to commission a luxury yurt.

The interest on the whole of the £195,000 borrowed is an allowable deduction against the rental income, because it represents part of the cost (the market value of £300,000) of introducing the house into the business of property letting.

The same applies in the case where there is a delay between the purchase of a buy to let property and the first letting of it:

NOTE 1: This strategy only works if the total amount borrowed is no more than the market value of the property at the time it was first let. Once the property has been let, interest on borrowing against any further increase in its market value will be allowable only if that loan is used for a business purpose – for example, to fund the deposit on another buy to let property.

NOTE 2: The refinancing to release the equity does not have to be done before the property is let for the first time – it could be done at any time while the property is still let, but the limit for interest relief is the market value at the time of the first letting, not at the time of the refinancing.

NOTE 3: There can be traps for the unwary here – if for example the letting of the property makes a loss after expenses, then this may restrict the amount that can be withdrawn by the equity release. It is prudent (as Gordon would say!) to check with a Tax Adviser before refinancing and releasing equity in this way.

11 Furnished Holiday Accommodation

This is a special type of furnished letting, and it enjoys a number of tax advantages over the ordinary letting of furnished or unfurnished residential accommodation. We will look in detail at the advantages and the rules, but in summary, the advantages are:

- Capital allowances for furniture and machinery and plant in the property

- The income from the property counts as "earned income" for the purposes of making pension contributions

- Because the income is "earned income", the rule we have just looked at about property jointly owned by a married couple does not apply – they can divide the rent between themselves in any proportion they like

- If you sell the property, it will be treated as a business asset for CGT, so you may be able to claim Entrepreneurs' Relief, and you can claim Rollover Relief if you reinvest in another property (these reliefs will be explained later in this guide)

- If you make a gift of the property (to your children, for example) you can "hold over" the gain

- For Inheritance Tax, the property may qualify as "Business Property" but only in certain circumstances

11.1 So, what is "Furnished Holiday Accommodation?"

First of all, it has nothing to do with holidays. The tests are all to do with the type of letting, and the tenants do not have to be on holiday. In practice, it is likely that most tenants will be holidaymakers, but there is no need to make sure they are not doing any work during their stay!

In order to qualify as Furnished Holiday accommodation, a property must be:

- Available for short term (each let under 31 days) letting as furnished residential accommodation on a commercial basis to the public generally for at least 210 days in the year (so no offices, and no letting at a cheap rate to friends or family during this period), and

- Actually let on these terms for at least 105 days in the year,

The typical pattern is for there to be short term lettings for the spring, summer, and early autumn months, and then for there to be a longer term "winter let" from, for example, 1 November to the end of March, but this is not a rule – the 210 days can be made up of any days in the year, as can the 105 days.

11.2 Furnished Holiday Accommodation (FHA) in the European Economic Area

Furnished Holiday Accommodation in the European Economic Area that comes within the rules set out above enjoys the same tax privileges, but is treated as a separate property business from the UK holiday lets.

11.3 Capital Allowances

You can claim capital allowances on the cost of furniture and such items as cookers, fridges, and so on. (You will remember that for a normal furnished letting, these could only be dealt with by using the 10% Wear and Tear allowance and now Replacement Furniture Relief).

You can therefore claim the "Annual Investment Allowance" of 100% of the first £200,000 of expenditure each year on plant and machinery, and a writing down allowance at 18% per year on any balance of expenditure (8% on "integral features" such as plumbing and heating).

Note that you **cannot use the 10% wear and tear allowance for FHA. The Renewals Basis has been abolished by statute for all businesses except furnished lettings.**

11.4 Losses

Since April 2011, losses on FHA in the UK can be set only against other UK income from UK FHA, and the same will apply to losses on EEA FHA – they can only be set against income from other EEA FHA.

11.5 Pension Contributions

FHA income is treated as "earned income" for the purpose of making pension contributions to your pension scheme. This is probably less significant since the new rules for pension schemes came into effect in 2006, (that allowed modest contributions without needing relevant earnings) but it can still be useful.

11.6 Profit Split for Married Couple or Civil Partnership

Because the income is "earned income" the 50:50 rule referred to above does not apply to married couples – they can split the rental income between them in any proportion they agree.

11.7 Capital Gains Tax

This is where the most significant reliefs for FHA can be found:

11.7.1 Rollover relief

If you make a capital gain when you sell certain types of business asset, you can "roll over" that gain by investing in an appropriate new business asset, and FHA is one of those assets, while normal lettings are not:

David owns and runs a pub – he does not live on the premises, because we explained to him when he bought it that that would make this Case Study too complicated!

He decides he would like to retire and lead a quieter life, so he sells the pub for £500,000, making a capital gain of £250,000 (before entrepreneurs' relief – see later).

If he invests his £500,000 in ordinary letting property, he will not be able to postpone the CGT of about £24,000 on his capital gain of £250,000 (we will see how this works out when we come to entrepreneurs' relief).

If instead he invests the £500,000 in FHA (say in three holiday cottages), he will pay no CGT, because the gain will be "rolled over" into the FHA properties. Instead of the £250,000 gain being taxed, it is deducted from the cost of the holiday cottages so that when he comes to sell these, he can only deduct £250,000 (real cost £500,000, less gain rolled over £250,000) when he computes the gain on the holiday cottages.

He need not invest all the sale proceeds to get some rollover relief, but some of the gain will then be taxable. If he only spends £400,000 on the new cottages, the computation will be:

Sale proceeds	500,000
Less reinvested	(400,000)
Amount not reinvested	100,000
Amount of gain not reinvested (250,000 – 150,000)	100,000

So he will pay CGT on a gain of £100,000. It may in some cases be appropriate not to reinvest (say) £11,200, deliberately so as to use the CGT Annual Exemption. This may become more worthwhile, if there are joint owners.

There is a limited window of opportunity for reinvesting in this way.

The new asset must be bought during a four-year period which begins **one year before** the old asset is sold, and ends **three years after it is sold.** In some circumstances, the three-year limit after the sale of the old asset can be extended, but **do not rely on this without taking advice from a Tax Adviser first.**

Note 1: Because FHA is defined by how it is let, rollover relief will at first be granted conditionally on the basis that, provided the property is in fact used as FHA, the relief will be confirmed.

Note 2: If you subsequently occupy the FHA as your home, so that when you sell it you are entitled to some measure of relief from CGT (main residence), then the held over gain will be brought back into charge.

11.7.2 Gifts of Business Assets

Normally, if you make a gift of an asset, or sell it for less than its market value, you will be charged to capital gains tax as if you had sold it for its market value on the day you disposed of it.

If the asset is a "business asset", however, you can hold over the gain.

Normal investment properties are not "business assets" for this purpose, but FHA is:

Case Study - 29   Hold Over for Gifts of FHA

Some years after buying the FHA, David is getting on in years, and he decides he will make a gift of one of his holiday cottages to his daughter, Rosie.

After rollover relief across the three properties as above, the "CGT base cost" of this particular cottage is £100,000, but its market value is now £250,000. If this were not FHA, and David gave it to Rosie, he would make a capital gain of £150,000, on which he would pay CGT of about £39,000, but as it is FHA, he can "hold over" this gain.

He will pay no CGT, but Rosie's "cost" when she comes to sell will be reduced by the gain held over, so her cost will be £250,000 less £150,000 = £100,000.

In effect, Rosie acquires the asset at David's base cost: the gain on her eventual disposal will be David's postponed gain, plus the increase in value while Rosie has owned it.

12 Commercial Property

By "commercial property", I mean any property which is not residential property so, for example, offices, factories, shops, and warehouses would all qualify.

Most of what I have said about letting residential property applies to commercial property as well, but there are a few other points to bear in mind:

12.1 Capital Allowances

Unlike residential lettings, (except FHA), the landlord of a commercial property can claim capital allowances on the cost of plant and machinery. This can include:

- Heating / air conditioning
- Lifts
- Lighting and other electrical wiring
- Telecommunications and data infrastructure
- Washroom fittings, water supply, plumbing, etc.
- Kitchen fittings

It is often possible to claim a very substantial proportion of the cost of a commercial building – even one that has been held for a number of years – under the CAs rules. However, this is a very complicated and technical area, and you should take advice from a Tax Adviser if you are going to be incurring significant expenditure of this type.

In particular, if you are contemplating the purchase of a commercial property, you <u>must</u> include Capital Allowances in your negotiations with the vendor. If you do not, you may not only miss out on some very valuable tax reliefs yourself but you could "taint" the property for any future buyers as well.

Please refer to: http://www.property-tax-portal.co.uk/commercial_tax.shtml

12.2 Premiums for Leases

The rules for premiums apply to any lease of a property, but as they are more common in letting commercial property, I will deal with them here.

This is another highly technical area of tax, so what follows is only a very broad outline of the basic concept. If you are going to charge a premium for a lease, take advice!

A premium is a capital sum paid to the landlord in exchange for the landlord granting a lease to a tenant.

Because (generally) capital gains are taxed at lower rates than income, it would be an attractive idea to grant a lease at a very low rent, but with a high premium.

You would pay CGT on the premium, but there are various tax reliefs that could reduce the tax you paid to much less than the amount of the income tax you would have paid on the rent.

For this reason, there are special rules for premiums paid for the grant of a new lease of 50 years or less:

Case Study - 30   Premium for "Short" Lease

Aladdin has a warehouse to let, and Sinbad wants to lease it for 20 years. They agree that the rent will be £5,000 per year, and that Sinbad will pay Aladdin a premium of £30,000 on the day the lease is signed.

Because the lease is not for a period of more than 50 years, part of this premium will be treated as if it were rent paid by Sinbad, rather than a capital sum.

To find the amount, we use a percentage found as follows:

Deduct one year from the length of the lease: 20 - 1 = 19.

Multiply the result by 2: 19 x 2 = 38

38% of the premium will be treated as a capital payment.

This means that £30,000 x 38% = £11,400 will be included in a CGT calculation for Aladdin.

The remaining 62% of the premium will be treated as if Aladdin had received that much rent on the day he granted the lease to Sinbad.

62% of £30,000 = £18,600, so for the first year of letting, Aladdin's rental income from the warehouse (assuming the lease was signed on 6 April), will be rent of £5,000, plus deemed rent of £18,600 = £23,600.

From Sinbad's point of view, he can claim a deduction (assuming he is using the warehouse for a trade) of the actual rent he pays (£5,000), plus the amount treated as rent, spread over the length of his lease (£18,600 divided by 20 = £930 per year).

The taxation of premiums is highly technical, and there are many pitfalls – to take only one example, suppose that Aladdin's warehouse was not big enough for Sinbad, and they agreed that instead of paying a premium he would pay for the cost of building an extension to it.

This could be treated as a deemed premium, and Aladdin would be treated as if he had received a premium equal to the increase in the value of the property to him on the day the lease was signed.

Note that this would not necessarily be the cost of the extension – the question would be, what was the market value of the warehouse before Sinbad agreed to build an extension, and what was the value immediately after he agreed to do so?

We repeat: ask a Tax Adviser if you are getting involved with premiums for leases!

13 Entrepreneurs' Relief

This was introduced with effect from 6 April 2008, to replace the previous Taper Relief.

It is a lifetime allowance which taxes the first £10 million of eligible capital gains at a rate of only 10% instead of 28% (or 20% since April 2016, for **non**-residential property).

Unfortunately, it is only of limited relevance to property investors and developers, because it only applies to "Business Assets" – broadly, assets used for your trade, or shares in a trading company.

The two types of asset that will be of interest to the readers of this book which may qualify are:

- Furnished Holiday Accommodation – though you will need to show that what you are selling is a "part of a business". This can lead to highly technical arguments with HMRC, and expert advice is essential.
- Shares in a property development company – provided either:

    o You have owned them for at least one year, are a director or employee of the company, and own at least 5% of the voting shares, or
    o You have acquired **any** number of shares issued to you on or after 17 March 2016 and (will) have held them continuously for at least three years since 6 April 2016. (This is a new relief for long-term 'external' investors, announced in the 2016 Budget).

14 Stamp Duty Land Tax

Stamp Duty used to be part of everyone's life.

If you have an old (pre-1960) pack of playing cards, you will find that there is a "stamp" on the Ace of Spades, certifying that Stamp Duty has been paid. Certain legal documents – such as receipts – had to be signed over a Stamp – literally, over a postage stamp – and such things as medicine bottles, perfume, hats, and gloves all bore Stamp Duty. Stamp Duty was introduced by William and Mary in 1694, as a temporary tax to pay for the war against France ("to pay for the war" is a common excuse for new taxes – income tax was introduced in 1799, as another temporary tax, to pay for the Napoleonic War).

These days, Stamp Duty itself basically applies only to sales of shares, at a rate of 0.5% on the amount paid.

Stamp Duty Land Tax (SDLT) was introduced in 2003, and as the name implies, it is a tax on land transactions.

The rate depends on the amount paid for the property, and whether it is "residential" or not. April 2016 has seen some major changes:

- A second, higher, tier of rates for residential properties
- Commercial (non-residential) properties will now be charged on a progressive scale, rather than on an "all-or-nothing" or "slab" basis. This follows residential property, which moved to the progressive basis in December 2014
- However, the "sting in the tail" for commercial properties is the introduction of a higher rate for more expensive properties/transactions

14.1 Residential Properties

For residential property, the SDLT is charged in bands, rather like income tax, so for a home costing £260,000, the first £125,000 is not taxed, the next £125,000 is taxed at 2%, and the remaining £10,000 is taxed at 5%, giving a total SDLT payable of £3,000 as set out in the "Residential Property" column in the table below.

Unfortunately, as a residential property developer, (or a simple residential property investor), you will now be more interested in the "Higher Rate" column, introduced for purchases completed from 1 April 2016. A 3% 'surcharge' has now been introduced across all bands. While individuals may **replace** their main residence and pay SDLT at the lower rate, companies and developers who are individuals and who already have a main residence will now have to pay SDLT at the higher rate(s).

Band	Residential Property	Residential Property – Higher Rate
0 - £125,000	Nil	3%
£125,001 - £250,000	2%	5%
£250,001 - £925,000	5%	8%

£925,001 - £1,500,000	10%	13%
Over £1,500,000	12%	15%

Transactions under £40,000 consideration are not returnable to HMRC and are not subject to the higher rate.

14.2   Mitigating the New Higher Rate - Multiple Properties

There are two tax-saving devices open to those looking to acquire several residential properties in one 'job lot' – or perhaps to incorporate their existing business, where SDLT may also be in point.

14.3   Multiple Dwellings Relief (MDR)

This is a relief available where a taxpayer buys several dwellings at once. SDLT is generally charged on the total consideration paid, but MDR allows the buyer to apply the rate applicable to the average property price in a transaction – noting that the minimum rate under MDR is 1%. A single physical property may contain several "dwellings" (such as an apartment block), but advice should always be sought to ensure that MDR is correctly applied.

14.4   Mixed / Multiple Acquisitions

Aside from MDR above, if a transaction involves either:

- "Mixed use" property, with both residential and non-residential elements, or
- 6 or more separate dwellings

Then the potentially lower "non-residential property" rates may be used (Finance Act 2003 s 116 (7)). (See the Case Study below).

14.5   Commercial (Non/Residential) Properties

For non-residential property, (which includes commercial or mixed-use properties), the 2016 Budget has just introduced a similar regime, for freehold purchases and lease premium payments, as follows:

Rate	Non- Residential Property
Nil	0 - £150,000
2%	£150,001 - £250,000
5%	£250,001 +

In the case of other leases, the amount payable depends on the "Net Present Value" of the rent under the lease – this is a complicated calculation, best left to a tax adviser, or the HMRC website offers a "calculator" to work it out. Having established the Net Present Value, it is chargeable at:

Rate	Non- Residential Property Lease NPV
Nil	0 - £150,000
1%	£150,001 – £5,000,000
2%	£5,000,001+

Despite moving from the antiquated 'slab' system, (that applied the SDLT rate to the total consideration), the overall effect of the changes to SDLT on commercial property in Budget 2016 is to **increase** the net SDLT yield to the Treasury: the cost will fall for lower-value properties – favouring smaller businesses – but will increase for higher-value properties, because of the 1% rate increase on higher-value property.

Case Study - 31   Case Study – Multiple Residential Properties

---

Portia purchases 10 additional residential properties in one transaction, for a total of £3 million. The average purchase price is therefore £300,000. She is purchasing at least 6 residential properties in the same transaction, so she can choose whether to claim multiple dwellings relief, or to apply the non-residential rates.

Multiple Dwellings Relief:
The SDLT due, using the higher rates on the average purchase price of £300,000, is £14,000. (This would have cost just £5,000 per property before the new higher rates were introduced). This is then multiplied by the number of properties (10) to give the total amount of SDLT due - £140,000.

Non-Residential Rates:
The non-residential rates apply to the total transaction value - £3 million. Thanks to the hike in non-residential rates as well, this will now cost £139,500. Portia can save herself £500 using this route as against Multiple Dwellings Relief.

In the absence of either claim, however, Portia would be looking at a total SDLT bill of £363,750

14.6 "Chargeable Consideration"

SDLT is based on the "chargeable consideration" paid for the property, so in the case of a gift for no consideration, no SDLT will be payable, though there are some exceptions to this:

14.7 Debts (Including Mortgages)

If you make a gift of a property which has a loan secured on it, the person receiving the gift will normally assume responsibility for the mortgage. If you make a gift of half the property, then half the mortgage will go with it. This is "chargeable consideration" for SDLT purposes:

Case Study - 32   Gifts and SDLT

Mr Time owns one house worth £210,000 and Mr Chance (no relation) owns one worth £260,000. They agree to exchange houses, with Mr Time paying Mr Chance £50,000 "equality money".

Mr Time will pay SDLT of £3,000 because he "paid" £260,000, made up of his house worth £210,000 and cash of £50,000.

Mr Chance will pay SDLT of £1,700 because he "paid" £210,000, made up of his house worth £260,000 LESS the £50,000 paid to him by Mr Time.

14.8 Transfer to a Company

Where a property is transferred to a company, and either:

- The person making the transfer and the company are "connected", OR
- The company issues any shares in exchange for the property transferred

Then the company must pay SDLT on the **market value** of the property – even if the land is transferred by way of a gift for no consideration.

14.9 Exchange of Property

Sometimes one property is exchanged for another, with either no cash changing hands, or with one side paying "equality money".

Case Study - 33   Exchange of Property

Mr Time owns one house worth £210,000 and Mr Chance (no relation) owns one worth £260,000. They agree to exchange houses, with Mr Time paying Mr Chance £50,000 "equality money".

Mr Time will pay SDLT of £3,000 because he "paid" £260,000, made up of his house worth £210,000 and cash of £50,000.

Mr Chance will pay SDLT of £1,700 because he "paid" £210,000, made up of his house worth £260,000 LESS the £50,000 paid to him by Mr Time.

14.10 "Linked Transactions"

Where two or more transactions are "linked", SDLT is charged on the rate applicable to the total consideration involved.

Transactions are "linked" if they are part of the same scheme, arrangement or series of transactions between the same vendor and purchaser, or persons "connected" with them.

Case Study - 34   Sale of House and Garden

Mr and Mrs Meadowcroft want to buy a house from Mr Smart. The price is £280,000, which means SDLT of £4,000

Mr Smart suggests that if Mr Meadowcroft bought the house for £240,000, and Mrs Meadowcroft bought the garden for £40,000, Mr Meadowcroft would only pay SDLT of £2,300, and Mrs Meadowcroft would pay nothing at all.

Unfortunately, this will not work – because Mr and Mrs Meadowcroft are "connected" (being husband and wife), the two transactions are "linked", and so they will pay SDLT of £4,000 between them.

SDLT is payable by the purchaser of the property concerned, so it will be a cost for both buy to let landlords and property developers.

For the landlord, it is part of the cost of acquiring the property for CGT purposes, so when he comes to sell it, it will form part of the cost he deducts to arrive at his capital gain. For the property developer, it is part of the cost of his trading stock.

15 Tax Investigations

HMRC have the power to "enquire" into any tax return from a company, a partnership, or an individual. They do not have to give a reason for the enquiry.

Anyone in the property business may face an Enquiry – each Tax Office opens a certain number of random Enquiries every year.

Enquiries come in different forms:

"Aspect" Enquiries. These are the least serious type of Enquiry – though they have been known to develop into Full Enquiries as they progress. In an Aspect Enquiry, the inspector will ask questions about a specific issue in the return – a favourite example for a property business would be to check if amounts claimed for repairs to a let property are in fact improvements to it (that cannot be deducted from rental income). A common query for property developers would be whether or not projects in progress at the accounts year-end had been correctly valued, so as to recognise an appropriate level of profit

Many Aspect Enquiries are closed down with no penalties being charged – though this is not always the case if large or blatant errors are found – but there will be interest to pay on any additional tax that is collected, running from the date the tax would have been paid if the return had been correct in the first place.

"Compliance Visits". These are aimed at checking that the business has complied with its obligations under the various laws and regulations it is obliged to obey. A compliance visit can be arranged to check that you are keeping the appropriate business records generally, but most are more focused on particular aspects of tax compliance. For property businesses, the commonest are:

- **Construction Industry Scheme (CIS) compliance**
  The CIS applies to all property developers (but not normally to property investors), and requires them to check the credentials of all the subcontractors they use, and record all payments to them, while in some cases deducting tax from those payments.

- **PAYE and benefits in kind**
  A sole trader or partnership will only be liable to this type of Enquiry if it has employees. The Enquiry will check if the business has operated PAYE correctly, and if all benefits in kind and expenses payments have been correctly reported on the annual Forms P11D.

- **VAT**
  HMRC will (for example) check that any property purchases have been handled correctly where there are Transfer of a Going Concern issues and that options to tax have been put in place properly on commercial buildings. A business that is "partially exempt" (see the paragraph on VAT in Part 10) is also likely to receive the occasional VAT visit.

  Full Enquiry
  This is the type of Enquiry that is generally referred to as a Tax Investigation, and it will involve the inspector looking at all the business accounts and records, and in some cases the private bank statements, etc., of the proprietors. It may also involve some or all of the more specialised types of Enquiry referred to above.

This is not the place for a detailed examination of how to deal with a tax investigation, but there is one vital piece of advice – **do not attempt to deal with it yourself!** In particular, if you receive a notice from the tax inspector to say he has decided to "Enquire" into your return, **seek professional help immediately** – in the first instance, from your accountant, though in serious cases he may well want to call in tax specialists like us.

If it is found that tax has been underpaid, then penalties may be due.

There is one other kind of investigation to consider.

This is where HMRC believe there has been serious tax fraud. In these cases, they will send you a "Contractual Disclosure Form" under Code of Practice 9 ("COP 9"). If you are ever sent a CDF, it is ABSOLUTELY ESSENTIAL to take expert advice from a suitably experienced Tax Adviser **immediately**.

UNDER NO CIRCUMSTANCES try to handle this yourself, and, at the risk of offending the profession, it is unlikely that your regular accountant will have the expertise to deal with a CDF investigation.

To end this part, here are the golden rules for dealing with tax enquiries:

- DON'T try to handle it yourself – get advice before you reply to the initial letter from the inspector, and at all costs DON'T ring the inspector up to "have a chat and sort this out"

- DON'T ignore it and hope it will go away – remember the mitigation of penalties for co-operation and disclosure

- DO be honest and upfront with your Tax Adviser – only then will he be able to help you

- DO talk to your accountant about taking out insurance to cover the fees for a tax investigation – the professional fees can be very expensive

16 Inheritance Tax for Property Developers

If you are a property investor or a property developer, you need to consider the impact of inheritance tax (IHT).

As we shall see, IHT can be more of a problem for the property investor than it is for the owners of other types of business.

There is a common misconception that IHT is only chargeable when someone dies. In fact, as we shall see, it is also chargeable in certain cases during your lifetime – but this is not always a bad thing!

16.1 IHT – The Basics

IHT is charged on "transfers of value". The commonest "transfer of value" is a gift, but as we shall see, there are other things which, sometimes unexpectedly, are transfers of value.

When a person dies, they are charged to IHT as if they had made a transfer of value of everything they owned on the day they died. In addition, any transfers of value they made in the seven years ending on the date they died are included.

IHT is charged at the following rates for 2016/17, depending on whether the transfer of value was made during a person's lifetime, or on his death:

Transfer of value	Death Rate	Lifetime Rate
0 – 325,000	0%	0%
Above 325,000	40%	20%

The first £325,000, which is charged at 0%, is called the nil rate band ("NRB"). It is often referred to as an "exemption", but this is a misleading way to think about it, as we shall see.

Not all transfers of value attract IHT when they are made. A simple gift from one individual, during his or her lifetime, to another will be a "potentially exempt transfer" ("PET"). This means that if the individual making the gift lives for another seven years after making it, it will fall out of account and no IHT will be charged on it when the individual dies. If, however, they die within seven years, it will form part of their estate at death:

Joe is a middle aged widower. On 1 April 2015, he makes a cash gift to his son of £100,000, to help him buy a house. This is a PET for IHT purposes, and so there is no IHT to pay at the time. Sadly, during 2015, Joe is killed in a car crash. His estate at death, after deducting all debts, is worth £250,000.

Because Joe has not survived for seven years after making the gift to his son, the PET is added to his estate when calculating the IHT:

Value of estate at death	250,000
Add gifts in last seven years	100,000
Total	350,000
Deduct NRB	(325,000)
Chargeable to IHT at 40%	25,000

A gift is only a PET if it is really given away. If the person making the gift continues to enjoy a benefit from it, it will be a **"gift with reservation of benefit" ("GWROB").** And will still be treated as owned by the giver, as we shall cover next.

The commonest example of a GWROB is where a parent gifts their house to their child, but continues to live there, but any gift which the giver continues to enjoy will be a GWROB:

Case Study - 36   GWROB

Sue is a widow, getting on in years, and like many otherwise modestly off people, she has one hugely valuable asset – her house. It is worth £350,000, and the mortgage was paid off long ago. The rest of her assets come to £200,000.

She made a gift of the house to her two children ten years ago, but has continued to live in it. Now she dies, still living in the house.

Because she "reserved a benefit" in the house, by continuing to live in it, for IHT purposes she is treated as if she still owned the house, so the value of her death estate is £550,000. It is irrelevant that she has survived for over seven years since she gave the house away – for IHT purposes it is still hers.

The GWROB rules were sometimes easy to get around, despite numerous tweaks to the legislation over the years. New rules were introduced around a decade ago, that tried to encompass GWROB scenarios. The effect of the relatively new "Pre-Owned Assets Tax" regime is that, if for some reason you are able to circumvent the GWROB regime, then you should – usually, but not always – be subjected to an annual Income

Tax charge, broadly based on the rental value of any asset that you continue to enjoy, having legally given it away. The rules for "GWROB" and "POAT" can be complex, particularly in their interaction with each other, and will happily catch innocent transactions where no avoidance was intended or realised. If you think that the rules may apply, then you should get advice.

Spouse Exemption

A gift or a legacy from one spouse (or civil partner) to the other is exempt from IHT. If you die and leave everything absolutely to your spouse, there will be no IHT to pay, and when their time comes, they will be able to double their nil rate band because your unused NRB has been transferred to them.

Business Property Relief (BPR)

For IHT purposes, "business property" gets relief at either 50% or 100%, depending on its nature. The crucial types of business property for property businesses are:

- An interest in a trading business

- Shares in an unlisted trading company

Unfortunately, a business that substantively includes investments (including investments in rental properties), or dealing in land, does not qualify for BPR.

The two types of business we have looked at in this guide that might qualify for BPR are:

- A property development business – the distinction is between an eligible business where the profits come almost entirely from the development or significant improvement of the property (property development, eligible for BPR), and one where the profit comes to a significant degree from astute buying and selling (dealing in land, and not eligible for BPR). Clearly, this can be a difficult distinction to make, and you should seek advice if you have any doubts as to which side of the line your business falls

- Furnished Holiday Accommodation – this does **not** automatically qualify for BPR, but where the owners are involved in providing services to the holidaymakers (either personally, or through a caretaker or a relative) beyond merely providing the furnished accommodation, then a good case can be made for BPR. If this relief is to be available, the lettings should be short-term only – typically weekly or fortnightly only. If the accommodation is let through an agency and there is no contact with the holidaymakers, the position is more doubtful.

  The way to look at it is – a hotel would qualify for BPR, and normal furnished lettings would not, so where on the spectrum between a hotel and a furnished letting does your property come? HMRC have recently started looking more closely at the level of services provided by the FHA, and are likely to challenge claims for BPR unless there is a high level of additional services – shopping, car hire, advice on local amenities, breakfast cooked for the guests, etc.

You will appreciate that many property businesses will not attract BPR, and so the value of the business is likely to be included in your estate on your death, unless you take steps to pass it on during your lifetime. The only good news is that any IHT due on your death which relates to land can be paid in ten annual instalments, rather than being due six months after your death, as is (broadly) the case with IHT on the rest of your estate.

The problem with making lifetime gifts is that the same assets that you would like to pass on (because they do not qualify for BPR) are the ones that you cannot claim holdover relief on (because they are not assets used for a trade), so if you make a gift of them to anyone except your spouse, you will be charged to CGT as if you had sold them at market value.

Fortunately, there is another way to get holdover relief. If a gift is chargeable to IHT as a "lifetime transfer", then any capital gain on that gift can be held over. This is where the "Nil Rate Band" for IHT becomes important:

Case Study - 37   IHT and Holdover for Gifts

Marcus is a widower, and he is not getting any younger, so he wants to pass on his buy to let property to his son, Tony. The property cost £150,000 in 1995, and its current market value is £350,000. There is a mortgage of £100,000 secured on it. If Marcus simply gave the property to Tony, he would be deemed to make a capital gain of £200,000, on which he would pay CGT of about £53,000 after his annual exempt amount.

Instead, Marcus sets up a trust, with Tony as the beneficiary, and transfers the property to the trust, on condition that the trust takes over the mortgage secured on the property.

In order to be a PET a gift must be to an individual, and a trust is not an individual, so the gift is a "chargeable lifetime transfer" for IHT purposes.

In order to find the amount of IHT payable, we look at how much Marcus' estate has reduced as a result of the gift. He is poorer by the value of the property (£350,000), but richer by no longer owing £100,000 on the mortgage, so the total loss to his estate is £250,000, and that is the amount chargeable to IHT.

Looking at the rates for IHT (see the beginning of this section) we find that the first £325,000 is charged at 0% (the "Nil Rate Band"), so no IHT is actually payable. Because the transfer is <u>chargeable</u> to IHT, however, Marcus (and the trustees of the trust) can make a claim to hold over the capital gain on the transfer. Marcus has used £250,000 of his £325,000 Nil Rate Band, but seven years after the date of this gift, it drops out of account and he can make another gift in a similar manner.

NOTE: Marcus makes the gift to "a trust". There are several different kinds of trust, and Marcus should take advice from a Tax Adviser before deciding what sort of trust to use. This is very much an area for experts, and there are likely to be disastrous consequences if you do not take specialist advice before embarking on a strategy of this nature.

There are other strategies for mitigating IHT, and property investors who want to be able to pass their properties down the generations need to take early advice on them – as you will have seen from Marcus, this sort of planning can be a long-term project, involving seven year gaps between transfers.

Congratulations – You've now finished 'Tax Secrets for Property Developers and Renovators'

To learn even more ways on how to legitimately cut your property tax bills please visit: www.property-tax-portal.co.uk.

Lightning Source UK Ltd.
Milton Keynes UK
UKOW07f0556170416

272306UK00003B/4/P